D0637711

SEVEN LIES ABOUT CATHOLIC HISTORY

SEVEN LIES ABOUT CATHOLIC HISTORY

INFAMOUS MYTHS ABOUT THE CHURCH'S PAST —AND HOW TO ANSWER THEM

DIANE MOCZAR

TAN Books
An Imprint of Saint Benedict Press, LLC
Charlotte, North Carolina

Copyright © 2010 Diane Moczar.

All rights reserved. With the exception of short excerpts used in articles and critical reviews, no part of this work may be reproduced, transmitted, or stored in any form whatsoever, printed or electronic, without the prior written permission of the Publisher.

ISBN: 978-0-89555-906-7

Cover design by Tony Pro.

Cover image: Spanish painting from the 1400s by Pedro Berruguete showing the miracle of Fanjeaux. According to the *Libellus* of Jordan of Saxony, the books of the Cathars and those of the Catholics were subjected to trial by fire before Saint Dominic. The Catholic books were rejected three times by the flames. Scanned from a history book. Wikimedia Commons.

Printed and bound in the United States of America.

TAN Books
An Imprint of Saint Benedict Press, LLC
Charlotte, North Carolina
2012

To Dr. William A. Donahue, founder and president of the Catholic League for Religious and Civil Rights, a champion debunker of both historical and contemporary lies about the Church. Excellent articles in Catalyst, the League's monthly publication, have dealt with some of the lies included in this book, as well as those concerning Pope Pius XII.

CONTENTS

Preface: Why Tell Historical Lies?   1

Introduction   5

1. The Dark, Dark Ages   11
2. The Catholic Church, Enemy of Progress   29
3. A Crusade against the Truth   53
4. The Sinister Inquisition   75
5. Science on Trial: the Catholic Church v. Galileo   103
6. A Church Corrupted to the Core   121
7. A Black and Expedient Legend   147
8. And There Are More . . .   163

Appendix 1: How to Answer a Lie   169
Appendix 2: Sources Used and Recommended   177

About the Author   190

ACKNOWLEDGEMENT

I wish to express my grateful thanks to Todd Aglialoro, my editor, for his professional guidance; I could not have completed this book without it. All those little conflicts over content, fights about footnotes, and tiffs about titles are now completely forgotten. Or almost.

PREFACE

_____

WHY TELL HISTORICAL LIES?

L ies about history are told, written, and passed down through generations for a variety of reasons. States create lies about rival states; an example of this is the Black Legend, invented mainly by England in the early modern period to blacken the reputation of its great rival, Spain. England's motives were political, economic (Spain had struck it rich in the New World while England had not), and religious (the Spanish king was the Catholic champion of Europe, whereas English monarchs were supporting the Protestant cause). More recently, anti-Catholic and anti-legitimist authors have told lies about the wartime regimes of Marshal Pétain in France and Franco in Spain. Communist writers lie about capitalism, capitalists about workers, and Renaissance historians about the Middle Ages. There can also be a real temptation to distort history for reasons of patriotism, or to cover up the failings of one's own party or religious leaders. (Catholics are not immune to this temptation.)

Historical lies, in short, are not necessarily told from religious motives, although religion is often one reason—sometimes the most important one—for their creation. In this book we will examine seven lies that do originate from religious motives and which have the Catholic Church as their target: either directly—as with the Inquisition, the Galileo case, the Church's alleged opposition to progress, the putative corruption of the Church before the Reformation, and the postwar attacks on Pope Pius XII—or indirectly, as with the Black Legend, the Crusades, and the Middle Ages.

In cases in which historical lies target the Church directly or exclusively, there are, again, a variety of specific motives for the attacks. Atheists are always happy to find some issue with which to discredit the Church, and ex-Catholics bearing a grudge against their former spiritual mother are often both rabid liars and prolific writers.

The most thoroughgoing and persistent religious historical lie seems to be the oddly unhistorical view that most Protestants take of pre-Reformation history. They posit an early Christian community of believers with a very loose ecclesiastical organization and no fixed hierarchical structure, only a couple of sacraments, and a few doctrines that fit whichever sect they belong to. This happy situation lasted, in their minds, until the Emperor Constantine stopped the persecutions and legitimized Christianity. Constantine supposedly reshaped the structure and doctrines of the Church by meddling in ecclesiastical affairs, and this Church-State coziness changed Roman Christianity into what became the bad Catholic Church we have today—while the true believers went underground in order to practice their pure and simple faith, only emerging into daylight with the dawn of the Reformation.

This scenario is incredible (in the literal sense) to anyone familiar with the mass of available early Christian documents and the history of the first three centuries. The myth survives mainly due to historical ignorance, as well as ideology, and the reason I do not deal with it directly in this book is that the cure for it is an entire course on early Western Civilization. Portions of this mythical history, however, will turn up in several of the following chapters.

INTRODUCTION

Y ou have undoubtedly come across some of the seven scenarios discussed in this book (and probably many more), all of which present Catholic history in an unfavorable light. Confronted with these assaults on the Catholic past, you may have recalled the spate of public apologies issued by some of the recent popes and decided that we Catholics have much to be ashamed of in the behavior of our ancestors. It might be better, perhaps you found yourself thinking, if we let all those dark centuries bury themselves and focused instead on an upbeat and non-confrontational future.

Importance of Understanding the Lies

The trouble with this attitude, other than the fact that it invokes yet another historical lie, is that the controversies do not go away. The rest of the world—history professors, textbook writers, filmmakers, media figures, Protestant apologists, anyone with an axe to grind against the Catholic Church—will not let us simply erase our past and go on. They continue to rake up their version of Catholic history, *ad infinitum*, and wield it with the intent of harming the Church. If we refuse to learn the reality of our history, we are reduced to twiddling our thumbs and looking sheepish when someone brings up the Inquisition, for example. When we do not know enough to refute the lies, we reinforce them by default—or we secretly buy into them ourselves.

We would do much better to confront the past of our Mother the Church objectively. History is God's acting in the world, most immediately through His own Church. Insofar as His fallible instruments are men, they can act ineffectively, stupidly, or maliciously, and thus affect history negatively. It very rarely happens, however, that the drama of Catholic history is performed exclusively by dumb, inept, or malicious Catholics. At critical moments, in fact, the actors are often saints—as we shall find in all seven historical periods that we shall examine.

We must keep in mind that although the Father of Lies is behind all lies, either directly or indirectly, any given purveyor of a lie may be completely unconscious that he is falsifying the historical record. There have certainly been rabidly anti-Catholic writers who deliberately distorted history to put Catholics and their Church in a bad light, but not all historical distortion is deliberate. For example, a historian may have a deep antipathy for monarchy—considered the most perfect and natural form of government during the Christian centuries—and therefore find it difficult to deal objectively with the historical manifestations of monarchy. The same goes for more recent authoritarian

Catholic governments, such as that of Salazar in Portugal. An economic historian sold on capitalism might find more to criticize in the guild system than would a less-biased researcher. And what feminists find to criticize in the Catholic centuries would take far too much space to go into here.

On the other hand, some historians distort history in the other direction, seeking to portray it as they would like it to be. Some romanticize the Catholic past to the point of ignoring real problems in the Church and the flaws of many Catholic historical figures. Then there is the bizarre case of John Boswell, a Catholic historian who died of AIDS in 1994. In works such as the book *Christianity, Social Tolerance, and Homosexuality*, he argued that the Church had formerly tolerated and even approved of perverse unions and had only changed its position in recent times. Boswell supported his thesis with a staggering collection of erudite footnotes to texts in several languages; only after his death did it come out that much of the book was based on the flawed work of his graduate student assistants.

The challenge for the Catholic historian, therefore, is to maintain an attitude of both objectivity and sympathy in dealing with the Catholic past as it truly was, based on competent and comprehensive research. More will be said about this difficult task in Appendix 1, but the first step is obviously to decide on a topic for study, assemble reliable sources on the topic or period chosen, and then devote the necessary time to studying them. Appendix 2 provides some reading suggestions, but there are many more good sources available, quite a few of them online. Even Wikipedia has some excellent introductory articles, with sources cited, including one on the new revisionism about the Spanish

Inquisition. Quite a few out-of-print but worthwhile volumes can also be found and read on the Internet.

Who Needs This Book?

Catholic apologists need it. They are usually not trained in history, and yet they find that Protestants of all stripes have an ingrained, distorted view of history that interferes with dialogue on doctrine. History is, in fact, vital to Catholic apologetics: "To be deep in history," wrote Newman famously, "is to cease to be Protestant."

Students need it just as much. After writing dozens of instructors' manuals, student guides, and test banks for numerous mainstream college history textbooks, my hair has ceased to stand on end at the lies embedded in these works. In only one or two instances have I been able to get an egregious error removed from a textbook, and even then the subtle bias of the work remained. I pity the many thousands of instructors and students who use these secular humanist and subtly anti-Catholic books without an antidote to the poison at hand. I hope this book may be an antidote.

Homeschoolers need it. Even if they have orthodox books to work with, some of these lies are not specifically addressed in them for want of space. And the additional resources this book provides will help develop the research skills of older students.

Ordinary Catholics need it, if they have ever come up against a negative argument about Catholic history that they could not answer. This book does not by any means answer all historical arguments, but it takes up those that are most prevalent and most insidious. When a non-Catholic friend spits out the word "Inquisition" and shudders expressively, one need no longer shudder with him. The reader of this book can say, "Oh yes, I was just reading about that. Let's talk about it." This does good to souls, as well as helping to strengthen our own appreciation for Holy Mother Church.

Why Call Them "Lies"?

I try to present each of these historical lies in its strongest formulation. In order to understand any controversy, we must try to get inside the opposing mentality and see the situation from that perspective. Only after we have understood the terms of the argument in their best and most persuasive forms can we evaluate it and determine whether it is true or false. So far, this sounds like the way anyone ought to deal with any historical question—for example, whether the Persian Wars would have been over sooner had the Greeks been more united. No one uses the word "lie" in describing differences of opinion on an ancient Greek topic, so why am I using it in the title of this book?

My reason for the negative characterization is that each of the positions we will examine has a dimension beyond the historical. Facts are neutral, but willful distortions of the facts are lies; and once the lies are articulated, they do not cease to be lies even when they are innocently repeated by those who are unaware of their mendacity. Thus we will have to disentangle, for each of our seven topics, the actual historical situation from the spin put upon it by those who have used it as a weapon against the Church, from its first appearance right down to the most recent college textbook author and movie maker.

My discussion of each lie is necessarily brief; full

treatment of each one would require one or more individual volumes for each topic. Fortunately, such work has been done or is in the process of being done on several of the lies, and I have included print and online resources for the reader to consult. If I succeed in enabling readers to spot these lies when they hear them, understand the truth behind the lies, and be armed with trustworthy sources for further information, my goal for this little book will have been achieved.

CHAPTER 1

THE DARK, DARK AGES

The Lie: The Middle Ages were one long Dark Age of ignorance and superstition, relieved only by the advent of the Renaissance.

The professor in the video is from a prestigious university in California. The video is one of a series of films made for distance learning in numerous colleges some years ago and also shown on television. The lectures are illustrated, and for the medieval segment most of the pictures are dark and grotesque to reinforce the idea that the Middle Ages were "dark." The professor even observes that in the Middle Ages, when the sun went down, it got dark outside: picture of dark village on the screen. When he gets to medieval people, he refers repeatedly to the "awkwardness of their minds." They were so awkward that they built buildings that fell down: painting of a building—actually dating from a later period—that has crumbled to the ground.

Just when the medievalist viewer, writhing in front of the screen, is muttering, "What about the cathedrals, you idiot!" and looking for a brick to heave through the TV, the professor admits that the period also produced cathedrals—and that their foundations went down the depth of a subway station and their spires soared hundreds of feet. Then he asks how, if their minds were so awkward, could medieval people have produced such beauty? Answer: to *compensate* for the awkwardness of their minds. We must also not forget that these awkward ignoramuses rarely even knew what time it was, since their sundials could not work in the dark. Apparently the professor had never heard of water clocks. (Needless to say, there is no mention of Thomas Aquinas, Roger Bacon, Bonaventure, Duns Scotus, or any other reasonably bright medieval thinker.)

Anti-medieval prejudice is built into our culture. A reporter covering a civil war in a primitive society will inform us that the participants exhibit "medieval barbarism." Discussion of a bizarre cult will often include references to "medieval superstition." Then there is "medieval torture," used to describe really bad atrocities. Where did this view come from, and is it true? After all, if there is smoke, there must be fire somewhere, somehow, must there not?

Renaissance authors, Enlightenment *philosophes,* popular writers, and anyone who dislikes on principle any period strongly influenced by Christianity have all contributed to the "black legend" about the Middle Ages. In recent times, however, historians of the Renaissance have probably been the most persistent scholarly promoters of the lie. Enamored of their favorite historical period, they are fond of trying to show how wonderful it was by contrasting it with the bad old days that preceded it.

The First Lies about Medieval Times

This approach did not, of course, originate in the twentieth century but in the fourteenth, when the first Italian "humanists," the original Renaissance men, began to idealize the classical culture of ancient Greece and Rome. In order to exalt that culture and to magnify the significance of their own literary work, they deprecated the culture of the more recent past as deplorably backward and insufficiently concerned with the real world. From there on the Middle Ages became, as we will see, a football for men of many persuasions to kick. Many writers since have disparaged the medieval period out of sheer ignorance or due to a naïve reliance on the opinions of the Renaissance writers. It should be noted here that most of those first humanists were Catholic, and that although some were critical of the Church and others were interested in introducing heterodox religious ideas, in most cases their disparagement of the Middle Ages did not spring from an animus towards Catholicism but from an exaltation of their own time, with its new artistic and literary styles and its optimistic view of man.

The fourteenth-century writer Giovanni Boccaccio thought that poetry had been dead until it was brought to life by Dante in the new age of "rebirth" that had just dawned. Dante was really, of course, a man of the Middle Ages in faith and mentality. He had even been born in the mid-thirteenth century, which was certainly one of the greatest medieval centuries. Nevertheless, Renaissance writers extolled both Dante and Giotto, Dante's contemporary, as "modern," while in the process—in numerous writings and with endless repetition—heaping scorn on all other medieval art, architecture, and thought. This attitude of men who were so convinced of the glory and superiority of their own historical period influenced the later writers who admired it too.

According to Professor Douglas Bush, the anti-Catholic prejudices of sixteenth-century Protestants and eighteenth-century Enlightenment writers also contributed to anti-medievalism. The anti-Catholic Voltaire, as might be expected, thought that "real philosophy" did not blossom until the end of the "bright" sixteenth century. Bush gives the most credit for shaping the anti-medieval lie, however, to the secular-humanist rationalism of nineteenth-century authors. He explains, "From that point of view, the Middle Ages appeared as not much more than a long cultural lag, a period in which man was enslaved by a system based on religious superstition and unnatural restraint." This view is illustrated, among many to choose from, by the works of Michelet and Symonds.

Nineteenth-Century Bashers of the Middle Ages

Jules Michelet (1798-1874), a French liberal historian, exalted the Renaissance as a heroic period of rediscovery of man and the world after a deplorable "dark" age. He offered an architectural analogy, contrasting the Gothic style, "which still supports the temple only with the aid of a cumbrous apparatus of props and buttresses," with the "rational, mathematical, self-supporting structural art" of the Renaissance. As for medieval science Michelet claimed that, "It exists thanks only to the enemy, to the Arabs and the Jews. The rest is worse than useless." He believed that both nature and science had fallen victim to medieval "terrorism" and repression.

Michelet had enthusiastic followers, including Jacob Burckhardt, whose celebrated *The Civilization of the Renaissance in Italy* was first published in 1860 and has been translated and reprinted many times since. The Renaissance could hardly have had a more zealous champion—at the expense of the Middle Ages. Using phrases from Michelet, Burckhardt gushed, "To the discovery of the outward world the Renaissance added a still greater achievement, by first discerning and bringing to light the full, whole nature of man." He characterized this investigation as "worldliness," which for him meant a quality of earnestness so modern that it could never be dislodged. "The Middle Ages, which spared themselves the trouble of induction and free inquiry, can have no right to impose upon us their dogmatical verdict in a matter of such vast importance." (Never mind his own "dogmatical" verdict!)

John Addington Symonds, a nineteenth-century literary critic who also was much enamored of the Renaissance, characterized the Middle Ages as a time when "man had lived enveloped in a cowl. He had not seen the beauty of the world, or had seen it only to cross himself and turn aside and tell his beads and pray." He then described St. Bernard passing by the shores of Lac Leman without noticing the loveliness of his surroundings but merely "bending a thought-burdened forehead over the neck of his mule; even like this monk, humanity had passed a careful pilgrim, intent on the terrors of sin, death, and judgment, along the highways of the world, and had scarcely known that they were sight worthy, or that life is a blessing. . . . Ignorance is acceptable to God as a proof of faith and submission; abstinence and mortification are the only safe rules of life: these were the fixed ideas of the ascetic medieval Church."

Fortunately—in his view—these depressing rules were destroyed by the Renaissance, "rending the thick veil which they had drawn between the mind of man and the outer world, and flashing the light of reality upon the darkened places of his own nature. . . . The Renaissance was the liberation of the reason from a dungeon, the double discovery of the outer and inner world." Well, it's pretty plain where he stood, and he was far from alone.

A Shift in Attitudes

There was an alternative nineteenth-century view of the Middle Ages that began to emerge in the early part of the century due to the work of scholars who collected and studied medieval texts previously unavailable. The new information from these texts suited those who favored Romanticism, an artistic and intellectual movement that reacted strongly against both Enlightenment ideas and Classical artistic norms. In particular, Romanticists disliked the denigration of the Middle Ages that was then in vogue. Their view of the Middle Ages, however, did not get much closer to the truth. As Jewish medievalist Norman Cantor writes in his *Inventing the Middle Ages*,

> The romantics of the early nineteenth century replaced
> this negative view of the Middle Ages with the shining

image of a Gothic culture steeped in idealism, spirituality, heroism, and adoration of women. But the romantics lacked the scholarship, the learning and instruments of research, to go beyond the most superficial kind of inquiry into the medieval past. Both the Renaissance denigration of the Middle Ages and the romantic acclamation of medieval culture were almost exclusively based on mere ideological projects. The romantics liked the Middle Ages because they thought they saw in that world the beliefs and behavior that contrasted vividly with the rationalism of the Enlightenment, the mechanism of the Industrial Revolution, and the centralizing bureaucracy of the national state, which they found repulsive and conducive to dehumanization.

In the second half of the nineteenth century, other movements such as nationalism, determinism, and social Darwinism began to influence the Victorians, and Romanticism waned. Cantor was moved to wonder why this era simply could not get the Middle Ages right: "Did the nineteenth-century historians misunderstand the Middle Ages because they were early pioneers who worked with a very narrow data base? Or was there something about the Victorian mind—its love of huge entities, vulgarly simple models, hastily generalized and overdetermined evolutionary schemes—that made it unsuitable for doing lasting work in interpreting the Middle Ages? We may say that both conditions were at work in fostering the Victorian misconstruction of the Middle Ages."

Perhaps the twentieth century would abandon this misconstruction? Certainly medieval studies became more popular with academics in the early part of the century, and the research of medievalists was beginning to turn up documentary evidence previously unknown or unutilized by historians. By the middle of the century, a number of first-rate works on various aspects of medieval thought and society had become available. The problem was that the writers of popular history had not yet gotten the word that there were good things to be found in those "middle" centuries.

Twentieth-Century Critics

Excellent academic work in medieval history was being done throughout the twentieth century, resulting in many excellent scholarly works that were available to anyone who took the trouble to look for them. They ranged from studies of daily life in the Middle Ages to medieval science and technology, to literature, art, and philosophy. That these sources seemed to be ignored by the writers of popular books of history is exasperating. Instead, popular twentieth-century books are filled with rehashing of the same tired falsehoods.

Here is John R. Hale, the author of the 1965 *Renaissance* volume in the Time-Life series, describing the Renaissance mentality as contrasted with the medieval: "Men and nature were treated not as generalizations of themselves, but as individual beings and things, interesting for their own sake." The implication would seem to be that medieval people saw all things as abstractions, and uninteresting abstractions at that. Two pages later we are told that Renaissance people wanted "a more practical kind of education than the one provided by the theological studies of the Middle Ages" and that "teachers turned their backs on the medieval idealization of poverty, celibacy, and seclusion, and instead praised family life and the wise use of riches . . . now the teaching of the church was not necessarily of a killjoy nature."

Even Catholic author Anne Freemantle displays the prevailing attitude toward medieval civilization in her contribution to the Time-Life series, *The Age of Faith*, asserting that medieval intellectual life paved the way for the Renaissance—that is, that the culture of the Middle Ages was merely a stage on the way to a *really* great period. She could find nothing good to say about the Crusades, yet the Moors in Spain are said to have had a culture that was "broad and tolerant," and supposedly the great tenth-century scholar Gerbert adopted "the inquisitive, questing spirit of Moorish scholarship." I suppose he had to get an inquisitive spirit from the Moors because there was no such thing as scholarship in Christian Europe.

Nearly thirty years after the appearance of the Time-Life books, bashing the Middle Ages was still a popular indoor sport for writers, as shown by William Manchester's *A World Lit Only by Fire: The Medieval Mind and the Renaissance: Portrait of an Age.* Manchester was a journalist, not a trained historian (though he wrote historical biographies, books on World War II—in which he had served—and other works.) While scholars carped, Manchester's books sold; apparently his publishers did not mind that what he wrote was false.

Manchester's view of the Middle Ages had few nuances. According to him, in medieval times the strongest characteristic of the Catholic religion was complete resistance to change. People not only did not know what time of day it was, they also had no sense of historical time. Medieval culture—what there was of it—could not compare with that

of the classical ages or with the culture of today. As for the
Church, it was a disaster, riddled with corruption, superstition, and worldliness.

Difficulties in Confronting the Lie

I have been fighting this lie since I first started teaching
and writing. Semester after semester I have pointed out to
my students the lies about the Middle Ages in the various
textbooks my college has required, hoping that somehow
my lectures and online notes would be able to penetrate
the great wall of rigid student principles, one of which is:
"If it's in the book, it must be true." Term after term I have
knocked myself out explaining the bias that still permeates
much of what is written about this great period.

Sometimes I give the myth first, carefully explaining that
what I am saying is merely what they will be reading in
their books, *not* what truly reputable scholars in the field
have to say. This is tricky, because a sizable portion of the
class will usually start taking down the myth in their notes,
on the principle that what the professor is saying might be
on the test—and I have to holler, "Don't take this down!
It's not true!"

Once in a while, of course, the truth does get through. I
recall one class in which I discussed the myth as presented
above, and a student came to me the following week to say
that he had gone to his literature class after our history ses-
sion and heard the professor saying almost exactly what I
had said—except that she was stating the lie as the truth,
whereas I had explained why it was a lie. "I sat in the back
and laughed," he said. At least that one student got the point
I was trying to make, but it is discouraging to realize that

many professors often shy away from confronting historical lies. The solution of one colleague to such controversies is simply not to teach the Middle Ages at all. He skips
ahead to the congenial Renaissance and avoids the whole
subject. The problem is that all those errors and prejudices
about the Middle Ages have by now seeped so deeply into
the popular culture that it will take considerable effort to
eradicate them.

Fortunately the tide has begun to turn, among scholars
if not yet among popular writers. There was a real renaissance—in the proper meaning of the word—of interest in
medieval studies in the late nineteenth and early twentieth centuries. By then, scientific medieval history, with its
emphasis on systematic collection and analysis of documents and other historical data, had become an organized
discipline. This development came a little too late to squash
the Renaissance myth before it got going, but it provided a
solid foundation for the flourishing of medieval scholarship
in most countries of the West. English and American historians such as Charles Homer Haskins, Lynn Thorndike, Dom
David Knowles, Richard Southern, Christopher Dawson,
Eleanor Shipley Duckett, Régine Pernoud, and many more,
both Catholics and non-Catholics, have helped to demolish
the lie. One recent college history textbook actually stated
that there was no real rupture between the medieval and
Renaissance periods, and no "dark age" at all: in fact, the
Renaissance was *not* superior to the ages that preceded and
followed it.

Achievements of the Middle Ages

This is a breath of fresh air for which we must be grateful, though it is still rare to find it in the mainstream academic world. One of my own professors—a Renaissance and Early Modern man—actually told me that if I could find a really significant contribution made by the Middle Ages, such as the concept of individual natural rights, that would prove it was a great period. (Otherwise, apparently, he could not find much good in the Middle Ages.) Individual natural human rights are considered one of the great contributions of the glorious Enlightenment of the eighteenth century, so the professor thought he was on safe ground in asking such a thing of the miserable Middle Ages. Well, what do you know; a few years later, medievalist Brian Tierney's *The Idea of Natural Rights* traced this concept back to *medieval* philosophers, including St. Thomas Aquinas.

A rousing good start to this welcome revisionism was made by Homer Haskins in his 1927 classic, *The Renaissance of the Twelfth Century*. The first lines of the preface throw down the gauntlet to the bashers of the Middle Ages: "The title of this book will appear to many to contain a flagrant contradiction. A renaissance in the twelfth century! Do not the Middle Ages, that epoch of ignorance, stagnation, and gloom, stand in the sharpest contrast to the light and progress and freedom of the Italian Renaissance which followed? How could there be a renaissance in the Middle Ages, when men had no eye for the joy and beauty and knowledge of this passing world, their gaze ever fixed on the terrors of the world to come?"

In truth, he continues, "The Middle Ages exhibit life and

color and change, much eager search after knowledge and beauty, much creative accomplishment in art, in literature, in institutions." However, "This conception runs counter to ideas widely prevalent not only among the unlearned but among many who ought to know better. To these the Middle Ages are synonymous with all that is uniform, static, and unprogressive: 'mediaeval' is applied to anything outgrown . . . The barbarism of the Goths and Vandals is thus spread out over the following centuries even to that 'Gothic' architecture which is one of the crowning achievements of the constructive genius of the race." On the other hand, he adds, those who speak of the "enlightenment" of the Renaissance must ignore the Renaissance preoccupation with such unenlightened pursuits as alchemy and demonology.

Haskins's seminal work demonstrated the twelfth century's tremendous interest in learning and education and its revival of the intensive study of the Latin language and classical literature. These had declined in the previous period, following their earlier cultivation in Charlemagne's empire. Science, philosophy, jurisprudence, and historical writing all underwent revivals in the twelfth century, while masterpieces were produced in every artistic field.

Perhaps most notably, the first new architectural style in seven hundred years was developed: the Gothic. Gothic structures had walls soaring into the sky and numerous windows to let in so much light that some of the buildings—like the Sainte Chapelle in Paris—seem to have no walls at all. In a real innovation, the walls were supported from the outside by those "flying buttresses" that Michelet so disparaged. In this connection, Chesterton called medieval civilization "a great growth of new things produced by a living thing," contrasted with the Renaissance as "a resurrection of old things discovered in a dead thing [the ancient world]." He went so far as to call Renaissance architecture "the Relapse," since it was not a new creation like the Gothic but a harking back to the domes of Rome.

As for social progress, the Renaissance is supposed to have brought improvements and refinements unknown to the loutish Middle Ages. But, as Christopher Dawson writes in *The Dividing of Christendom*, the Renaissance aristocratic ideal of life as a fine art brought "a growth of class differences and a loss of that unity of outlook which united a medieval king like St. Louis with the humblest of his subjects." That unity of outlook among ruler and ruled, and among all classes, was a precious thing to lose, as the future history of Europe would demonstrate.

Medieval People and Nature

The following chapter of this book includes a discussion of the medieval Church and medieval innovations in education, science, and technology, but something should be said here on the subject of how medieval people looked at nature. The bashers so harp on the supposed indifference of medieval people to beauty and to the world around them that one might well think there must be something to that claim. The Renaissance crowd, including Petrarch himself, makes a big deal of his climb up Mount Ventoux as some sort of milestone, so very Renaissance-y. Medievalists know, however, that a medieval Parisian schoolman had earlier visited that same mountain and even noted its altitude; medieval Germans of the tenth and eleventh centuries were also fond of climbing and describing mountains. As Lynn Thorndike observed, the only thing "Petrarch's account proves is his capacity for story-telling and sentimental ability to make a mountain out of a molehill."

In fact, the art of the Middle Ages is full of evidence that people observed nature very closely: the flowers and herbs that appear in medieval pictures and sculptures, for example, are so accurately reproduced that they can still be identified. Study of garden plants resulted not in purely utilitarian plots of herbs, but lovely landscapes that delight the eye. Medieval people had a keen sense of the beauty of natural things and a curiosity about them: they considered that beauty is a quality created by God to draw our minds to Him. Thorndyke observes, "The Middle Ages, so often said to have little love of nature, in point of fact gazed at every blade of grass with reverence."

Of course, as Thorndyke also observes, regarding the close-mindedness of Renaissance historians, "But what is the point of questioning the Renaissance?...So often as one phase of it or conception of it is disproved . . . its defenders take up a new position and are just as happy, just as enthusiastic, just as complacent as ever." This is particularly discouraging when the Church itself is in question.

Anti-Catholic Prejudice among Medieval Historians

I have taken pains to point out the many types of anti-medieval prejudice in order to show the variety of views that motivate such bias. But sometimes the motive is plain, blatant anti-Catholicism. It is gratifying to report that Norman Cantor incisively dissected William Manchester's book-length diatribe, referred to above, in a 1992 *Washington Post* book review. Referring to Manchester's obvious disdain for the Middle Ages, Cantor remarks, "Although the great medievalists David Knowles and Richard Southern are listed in Manchester's bibliography, he apparently doesn't believe a word they ever wrote on the astonishingly high degree of cultural creativity in the Middle Ages, certainly the equal of Roman achievement." On Manchester's characterization of the medieval Church as totally resistant to change, Cantor explains that the Church not only experienced many changes, but also "contributed to major advances in political and legal thought and practice. The Church was often in the vanguard of change in medieval Europe." To Manchester's claim that medieval people lacked "ego," Cantor states that self-consciousness and individuality were in fact central to twelfth-century culture.

We will never be able to destroy the anti-medieval view—which is not unique to Manchester—because it is often based on a hatred of religion and of the virtue of self-control that is beyond the ability of historical facts to affect. Cantor refers to one passage in Manchester's book as "a distressing revival of the worst kind of nineteenth-century anti-Catholicism," and he takes issue with that author's discussion of the Renaissance and St. Thomas More: "After a few generous words on Sir Thomas More, Manchester denigrates this refined thinker and heroic defender of conscience as 'a rigid Catholic.' Erasmus, of course, in Manchester's view, was a good guy because he attacked the clergy and made fun of popes."

The concluding paragraph of the review includes this sobering assessment: "It is distressing to think that this anti-Christian diatribe, reviving the wildest and most ignorant nineteenth-century polemics against the Catholic Church, will with the publisher's heavy promotion make its way into thousands of middle-class households and school libraries." Cantor then recommends a number of films set in the Middle Ages on which the reader might better spend the price of the lousy book.

Among researchers, the prospects for myth demolition are looking up. Hot topics now include the debunking of the alleged static and anti-progressive character of medieval culture, of the Crusades, and of the Inquisition.

In the following three chapters of this book we will deal with specific issues that are particularly dear to the bashers of the Middle Ages, whatever their stripe.

CHAPTER 2

THE CATHOLIC CHURCH, ENEMY OF PROGRESS

The Lie: With the rise of Christianity, European cultural and material progress in every field was retarded by religious opposition.

I n all historical periods, from Roman times to the present, we have heard the same refrain: the rigid, authoritarian Church keeps people from reading, thinking, and doing what they want. Even in the early days of Christianity, Tertullian was unwittingly laying the foundations of this lie. "What has Jerusalem to do with Athens?" he wrote. "I have no use for a Stoic or a Platonic or a dialectic Christianity. After Jesus Christ we have no need of speculation, after the Gospel no need of research." He eschewed philosophy, "with its rash interpretation of God's nature and purpose.

It is philosophy that supplies the heresies with their equipment. . . . A plague on Aristotle."

This stifling of human liberty, so the lie goes, led to the suppression of creativity and prevented any sort of progress during the long Dark Ages of Christendom. During those many centuries the Church used the governments of Europe, which it controlled, to suppress freedom. Any dissent was stifled in the torture chambers of the Inquisition. Finally the lights went on again, because it was the Renaissance and there were finally free-thinking people like us—Machiavelli, for example. The monk Savaronola tried to stop the Renaissance through fanatical preaching and by burning the masterpieces of great painters, but he failed.

The Protestant Reformers, although a few of them were almost as fanatical as the Catholics, had the great merit of overthrowing the evil Church and breaking its stranglehold on states, people, and culture. Freedom was beginning to dawn! Thanks to martyrs like the great astronomer Galileo, who was imprisoned, tortured, and put on trial for proving that the earth goes around the sun, Science had begun to combat Catholic superstition.

The French Revolution was another step forward because monarchy—the repressive system promoted by the Church—was overthrown and people were finally given the freedom to think and do whatever they liked. The nineteenth and twentieth centuries reinforced this freedom by removing legal restrictions on homosexuality, abortion, contraception, and other exercises of human liberty, and by separating church and state so completely that Catholic puritanism was no longer inflicted on the citizens of most democratic countries. The demand for intellectual and moral freedom has been so powerful that even the papacy has caved in. It has abolished the Index of Forbidden Books, the Inquisition, and the Imprimatur, and has watered down the language of the few concordats that still exist with secular states. The papacy today rarely acts against even its most notorious heretics, who in a less enlightened age would have been burned at the stake. This demonstrates that the Church has finally realized how wrong it was in all those other centuries and that it has finally seen the light of liberal humanism.

Confronting the Lie

This one is particularly clever and formidable to deal with because so many of its components are drawn from reality: the believer's error is the atheist's truth. The key here is to distinguish truth from falsity, insist on a definition of terms, and identify the unspoken criteria that motivate purveyors of the lie. We can start by identifying the obvious errors of fact, bracketing those dealing with the Inquisition and the Galileo case since those are treated in separate chapters.

First to the early Church: it is true that there was a debate as to whether Christians, possessed of the fullness of supernatural truth, had any business pursuing secular studies. It is not true, however, that it was Tertullian's disparaging view of philosophy that carried the day for early Christians; rather it was that of St. Clement of Alexandria. This Doctor of the Church was a sophisticated intellectual, familiar both with classical philosophy and with the Christian learning—soon to become theology—that was then developing. Teacher, writer, devoted priest, Clement *defended* philosophy.

"The Greeks," he wrote, "should not be condemned by

those who have merely glanced at their writings." (One wonders whom he has in mind—Tertullian, perhaps?) St. Clement saw philosophy as "a clear image of truth, a divine gift to the Greeks." Certainly philosophy could not provide the whole of God's truth, but it could prepare the mind to receive it. St. Clement also believed that a learned man should "bring everything to bear upon the truth; so that from geometry, music, grammar, and philosophy itself he culls what is useful and guards the Faith against assault." This was the true mind of the great thinkers of the Church, from that day to this, and Clement's statements would become the program for Christian studies in all subsequent ages.

The Church and Education

So far was the Church from desiring docile, ignorant believers to manipulate for its nefarious ends, that from the very beginning it made education a priority. Catholicism was always an intellectual religion, and the faithful certainly desired their own schools, though early attempts to organize such schools did not succeed very well. As the Roman Empire drew to its close, therefore, Christians made do with the least objectionable pagan schools for subjects such as rhetoric, grammar, literature, philosophy, and the other subjects taught to Roman students. There were Christian schoolmasters in some of these schools, with specialized teachers for religious instruction. Meanwhile, religious education for catechumens was handled by educated clergy and could last for a year or two, until the prospective Christian was thoroughly grounded in the doctrines of the Faith as well as its moral principles and its precepts. After the fall of Rome, the Eastern Empire developed truly

Christian schools, though the West relied primarily on tutors employed by families or on wealthy older students, until the monasteries were at last able to take up the task of teaching. In sum, from the earliest period of the Church's history, education was a top priority.

With the beginning of the Dark Ages after the fall of the Western Roman Empire, there came a chaotic period of massive foreign invasion and breakdown in every area of life and culture. During this time of upheaval, civilization survived almost exclusively in one institution: the Catholic Church. The educated clergy were often the only men capable of handling the administration of the rapidly disintegrating cities and providing basic services to the population—while the cities dwindled into towns, the towns into villages, and urban life slowly disappeared from Europe. Among the many things lost in that "breaking of the world" was the knowledge of many scholarly disciplines, as well as of libraries and the artistic creations of the classical world. How is it, then, that we still seem to possess so much of that heritage today?

The answer is that almost all of what we have now was preserved by the Catholic Church. Only a few original manuscripts survive from the Roman period; what we have are copies, and those precious copies were made in the monasteries scattered throughout the former Roman Empire. As the level of literacy declined and schools disappeared along with urban life, learning was passed down from individual teachers to their students in the same informal way as early Christian parents had taught their children, and from one generation of monks to the next. The monastic libraries were built up by the efforts of monks who spent their lives patiently copying not just Church writings, but all the manuscripts they could find. It is even shocking to read some of the pagan material they preserved within monastic walls—which may indicate that some of the copyists did not fully understand what they were reproducing. They were driven by a desire to preserve a heritage they viewed as too precious to be lost, whatever its individual components may have been. Far from disparaging knowledge and learning, these monks of the Church dedicated their lives to furthering it.

One of the first to appreciate the necessity of copying manuscripts was the scholar Cassiodorus, who had had a long career in the service of a series of Gothic kings in Italy in the sixth century. He agreed with the views of St. Clement of Alexandria, and when he retired to the Roman monastery of Vivarium he encouraged the copying of both secular and religious manuscripts. He also wrote instructions for the scribes on how to do it right. He stipulated, "lest in performing this great service copyists introduce faulty words with letters changed, or lest an untutored corrector fail to know how to correct mistakes, let them read the works of ancient authors on orthography." Cassiodorus also recommended a special type of long-burning lamp for night work, as well as a water clock to mark the time of day and night. (This text alone shows that the idea that people never knew what time it was until the mechanical clocks of the Renaissance came along simply does not hold water...)

Catholic Re-establishment of Schools

Here and there within the monasteries of the Dark Ages, formal schools for the education of others besides religious began to emerge. In the course of centuries of chaos, monks and nuns had been forced into many roles their founders had not foreseen, such as nursing, and training farmers in new agricultural techniques—which led to advancements in knowledge. The cultivation of medicinal herbs in monastic gardens, for example, produced the first pharmacists— that is, monks.

Early on, monasteries had begun providing shelter for stranded travelers and had started adding guest quarters on their properties. Something more became necessary, however, the day a brother doorkeeper opened the monastery door and found a baby on the doorstep. Soon convents and monasteries found themselves setting up nurseries, orphanages, and then schools. St. Bede in England wrote about methods of teaching the very young, and these were apparently used in the elementary schools that Charlemagne— in the eighth and early ninth centuries—established all over his empire. His own palace school was headed by a renowned British monk and scholar, Alcuin of York, and Alcuin employed talented men of all classes and nationalities. These monastic schools were able to grow and expand far more once the barbarian invasions subsided in the late ninth century.

What did they teach in the monastic schools? Contrary to what might have been expected, these schools did not simply provide instruction in reading and writing or the rote memorization of prayers and religious doctrines. The accounts of curricula in even Dark-Age monastic schools show what a surprising amount of classical learning was available in the libraries of religious houses. It is true that during this period of barbarian raids and minimally literate monastic recruits, some of the texts in the libraries were little used or comprehended. (We have an exchange of letters between two Dark-Age scholars discussing the question of what a "right-angled triangle" might be.) Even at the worst of times, however, there were geniuses like St. Bede, who produced a prodigious amount of scholarly work using Latin texts, and even some Greek.

There seem to have been two tiers to early monastic education. On the one hand, boys from the countryside surrounding the monastery would be taught their letters, basic arithmetic, and enough Latin to follow the Mass and understand the Creed and other prayers. They learned both the fundamentals of the Faith and the practical skills needed in their state in life, while those with priestly vocations received whatever further training the monasteries could provide. Often this would not be possible in an isolated monastic house, so boys who wanted to be priests would be sent to the houses of bishops for instruction.

In many areas the training they got was barely adequate: at the time of Charlemagne we read of priests garbling their Latin so badly that they were getting sacramental formulas wrong. Charlemagne insisted that such priests be properly trained and that monks who copied and composed texts— including letters—should do so correctly. He commented in one of his own letters (dictated because, ironically, he himself never learned to write) that he was getting letters from monks full of "uncouth expressions" and that this had better stop, "lest perchance, as the skill in writing was less, so also the wisdom for understanding the Holy Scriptures might be much less than it rightly ought to be."

Students destined for government service or the Church

were taught a classical curriculum, a version of that used in ancient Greece and Rome and based on the Seven Liberal Arts. Knowledge of these arts had survived in the West in manuscripts—copied and recopied—of Boethius and other Roman scholars. The seven "arts" were divided into the trivium: grammar, rhetoric, and dialectic (logic)—and the quadrivium: arithmetic, geometry, astronomy, and music. For centuries following the fall of Rome, those students fortunate enough to get any sort of education had all they could do to wade through a version of the trivium: reading and writing, correct speaking, clear thinking. The quadrivium was taught when higher levels of education became feasible. The point here is that the Church was—as at all times in her history—one hundred percent committed to both formal education and to learning of all kinds.

Higher Education in the West

The first steps in the direction of the university system we have today were taken in the early Middle Ages, when bishops began to set up cathedral schools. These urban institutions were more advanced than the monastic schools, which were generally located in the countryside or in small towns. With the cessation of foreign invasion and the economic revival of the eleventh century—a turning point in European history—came the emergence of the first cities seen in Europe since the fall of Rome. The schools set up by the bishops of these new towns and cities, located near the spectacular new cathedrals, attracted students from the dioceses in which they were located, and often from further away. These schools offered more advanced curricula, and their faculties included scholars drawn to the new urban centers by their larger libraries and expanded opportunities for learning and teaching. The early scholastic philosopher Abelard (who deserves to be known for more than his tragic affair with his student Heloise) was one of the teachers at the cathedral school of Notre Dame in Paris.

It should be stressed that the ancient Latin literary classics—and later on Greek texts, usually in translation—formed a major part of the arts curriculum. What was read, memorized, commented upon, and analyzed in the schools was that large body of classical texts that had survived the fall of Rome in monastic libraries. It is therefore simply false to assert that the classical heritage was for a thousand years buried, ignored, consciously suppressed by the bad old Church—and only liberated by Renaissance scholars who had liberated themselves from the Catholic stranglehold on culture. (That view of Renaissance scholars is false too—those scholars were nearly all Catholic themselves.) The evidence is overwhelming that medieval students were steeped in the Latin classics; they learned to read them, imitate their style, memorize them. Cicero was a favorite. And when Heloise, inconsolable in her renunciation of Abelard, took the veil in a convent, she recited Latin verses as she walked down the aisle, and consoled herself later with reading the Stoic philosophers.

The Universities and Science

As the popularity of the cathedral schools grew and the demand for education began to exceed their capacity, a new institution emerged in the cities of the West: the university. One sometimes reads (in books by authors who should know better) that medieval universities taught only theology and were therefore not worth much in the modern perspective. In fact, only one of the original universities (Paris) was specifically devoted to theology. Others specialized in law (Bologna) and medicine (Naples), while the curricula in all schools included grammar, logic, rhetoric, mathematics, music and astronomy.

As the name implies, the universities would encompass *all* learning and would pioneer the study of new disciplines and new techniques of teaching and learning. These new institutions of higher learning were seen—as all medieval social organisms were—as reflections of the Mystical Body of Christ. They were bodies *(corpora),* or *corporations,* made up of teachers and learners. In some places the masters were in charge of the corporation, but in other places the students were: they actually imposed fines on professors who showed up late to class, for example.

Most universities, after organizing themselves in a rudimentary way within the boundaries of a city such as Paris, would obtain a papal charter granting authority and legitimacy to their new institution. An ignorant critic would chortle "Aha!" at this point, assuming that the bad old papacy was naturally concerned with suppressing free thought and imposing its rigid ideology on the schools. In fact, the very opposite was true. Universities were anxious to obtain papal charters in order to avoid coming under the authority of the city fathers of the places in which they were located. These city fathers could be unsophisticated folk, over-willing to suppress any hint of what looked like heresy in the free exchanges of opinion that flourished in the universities. There are numerous examples of such towns-folk attempting to censor the teaching at one university or another, only to be *overruled by the papacy*, which had granted the original charter and frequently intervened in such disputes on the side of academic freedom.

It is precisely to this papal defense of academic freedom that we owe the amazing creativity and progress of medieval scholarship. One is tempted here to compare that Catholic attitude toward scholarship with Reformation attacks on scholars such as Copernicus and Kepler, both of whom were protected and encouraged by the Catholic Church. (We will get to them in a later chapter.)

Examples of groundbreaking medieval scholarship would fill volumes. In philosophy alone, the work of Duns Scotus, Thomas Aquinas, Bonaventure, Abelard, and Albertus Magnus is staggering. In science, it was again Albertus Magnus (St. Albert the Great, teacher of St. Thomas) who was the first botanist since classical times. It was the Franciscan, Roger Bacon, who first developed the science of optics, mapping the parts of the eye with extraordinary accuracy. A practical application of the new work in optics was the invention—by whom is still not clear—of eyeglasses. Certainly the medieval scholarly community, more given to reading and studying than perhaps any previous generation, would have appreciated that device. As for more theoretical science, late medieval scientists in England began to explore the mathematical physics on which Newton was later to build.

Writing in the *Homiletic and Pastoral Review* in December 1996, Father Joseph de la Torre, a specialist in Thomistic philosophy, traces the origins of the great scientific breakthroughs of the sixteenth and seventeenth centuries. He demonstrates that they were in fact the consequences of the epistemological realism of the thirteenth-century philosophers, with St. Thomas at their head. "The Thomistic method," he writes, was the real cause of the scientific breakthrough, not the method advocated by Francis Bacon, or that of René Descartes (both in the seventeenth century,) since the latter reduced it to mathematical deduction (mistrusting observation and experiment,) and the former reduced it to pure observation and experiment, excluding mathematics. The real creators of the scientific breakthrough, such as Leonardo da Vinci, Copernicus, Galileo and Kepler, and, of course, Newton, followed the . . . golden rules formulated by St. Thomas Aquinas."

Medieval scholars produced masterful works on theology, political science, law, teaching techniques, and much more. They were willing to explore every aspect of reality because of their commitment to rational analysis and their confidence in human reason. For them, the intellect was the highest faculty of the soul, and the truths it discerns could not possibly contradict the truths of the Faith because God is the author of both. This whole sprawling, inquiring, intellectual movement, one of the major developments in Western civilization, was originated, fostered, encouraged, and protected by the Catholic Church.

Catholic Thought on Economics

The history of Catholic economic thought has still not received full treatment in the English language, allowing lies and misunderstandings to exist more easily. Medieval thinkers were certainly concerned with the economic issues, though these were relatively uncomplicated until the advent of long-distance trade and modern capitalism.

One issue with which they were concerned was the taking of interest on loans. From early Christian times this was condemned as "usury" and considered a sin against charity. The basic idea was that if a man was so much in need that he had to borrow money, he should not be taken advantage of by being made to pay interest on it. Some theologians also considered interest/usury as theft: the man in need of money was in effect robbed of part of it when he paid it back. In a very simple agrarian economy, this was reasonable and just.

As the medieval economy expanded, however, and cities emerged again in Europe for the first time since the fall of Rome, the situation had become much more complex. All kinds of businesses were developing in the new urban centers, merchants were traveling, and bankers were busier than they had ever been. The question of "usury" was again debated. St. Thomas held that it was just for a banker to charge a reasonable fee for his services and the administration of a loan, but not interest, and this was the general attitude of the Church. (Jews, oddly enough, were exempted from this prohibition and only forbidden to take "excessive" interest.) Money was considered a static commodity that was used up; if you had run out of money you might borrow some, which you would then spend on necessities. St. Thomas likened the charging of interest (in addition to the banker's fees) to charging a customer for a bottle of wine and then charging him again when he drinks it. Money, in short, was something to be spent on things one needed.

The perspective changed in the later medieval period. With the emergence of proto-capitalism and the notion of money as something that was not simply static but that could increase if invested, a number of theologians began to rethink the question. A man who borrowed a sum of money to invest in a commercial enterprise was taking a certain risk, as was the banker who lent him the money. It began to seem just to the banker to allow him to charge a reasonable rate of interest; he was not only risking the amount he lent, he was prevented from doing anything else—possibly more profitable—with the money until it should be returned. Money was now viewed as something that could be grown in profitable activity; thus interest could now be seen as the lender's proper share in the profitable activity of the sum he had lent.

This whole question of usury and interest demonstrates the constant concern of medieval thinkers with justice and charity in economic affairs, as well as in all other spheres of life. It thus reflects the concern of the Church with promoting economic progress and prosperity. This concern is reflected with great clarity in the medieval guilds, which clearly incorporated Catholic economic principles.

Applied Medieval Economics: the Guilds

The guilds of the Middle Ages, which developed in the new urban centers that emerged out of the Dark Ages, were associations of masters and apprentices in various trades. A shoemakers' guild would comprise master shoemakers and young men learning the craft. When an apprentice was considered ready to become a master, he was assigned the task of making a "masterpiece" that would be judged by the masters. If he passed the test, he might become a "journeyman," which literally meant that he went on a year's journey around his country, staying at guild houses in the towns he visited and learning what he could about different ways of plying the trade of shoemaking. (He must have had a very good time in the process!)

Back home, the new master could set up in business for himself or go into an existing shop. As a member of the guild, he was expected to operate according to ethical principles: he charged his customers a just price, and he paid a just wage to his workers; he offered for sale only good-quality merchandise; he kept reasonable hours of work and did not work on Sundays or holy days (of which there were a great many in the Middle Ages). The guild, furthermore, served a number of important functions for its members. The various guilds of a town, which included most skilled workmen such as carpenters, bakers, traders, shoemakers, and others, were important elements of their society. On the feast day of their patron saint they marched in procession to the church, arrayed in the symbols of their guild; they held banquets and other social functions for their members and families. They might donate a work of art to the local church or sponsor a young man (who perhaps began as an apprentice but was discovered to have more of a talent for book learning) for a year at a university.

The social services provided by the guilds were impressive. According to the statutes of a guild in Southampton, England, if a guildsman fell ill his fellow members would not only send him suitable food, they would visit him and relieve the family members by watching over him for a time. If he died, they helped with the funeral preparations. A member who could no longer work received a pension from the guild. Customers of the guilds were protected by quality-control standards, which specified, for example, that butchers and cooks were forbidden to sell anything but "wholesome and clean" food. The streets in front of the shops were to be kept clean. Guildsmen who violated any of the guild's regulations were subject to penalties ranging from fines to the pillory.

We have a little work by a thirteenth-century business-man, a merchant, in which he discusses how a man ought to behave in order to be successful in business. It is a delight-ful mixture of spiritual and practical advice, much of which is still relevant today, and it gives a glimpse into the mental-ity of a businessman seven hundred years ago. According to the treatise, the merchant should begin each day with Mass and should count Our Lord, Our Lady, and his favor-ite saint as his partners, to whom he must account in per-forming his various tasks. He must be polite and agreeable, but shrewd enough to scrutinize things carefully before he buys them, and he must be sure to have witnesses to any bargain. He should charge his customers a fair price, and if an object is flawed, he should not conceal the defect but offer the thing at a lower price. He should inform himself of laws that might affect his business, as well as study foreign languages; he should exercise to keep fit and should avoid becoming despondent. He must, of course, avoid occasions of sin; he should dress well, eat well, avoid getting angry, and be eager to learn whatever he can. He will be a go-get-ter, in short, but a virtuous one. No wonder the High Middle Ages were such a prosperous period.

Catholic Political Thought

Guilds also played a large role in town government, and in many places they were the first to organize the governmental system. The growth of towns was a phenomenon of the period following the Dark Ages when the barbarian invasions had ceased, the climate had become extraordinarily favorable, and economic and urban life began to re-emerge in Europe.

The system that had preceded this period of urbanization was feudalism—a sort of ad hoc means of survival during the centuries that followed the collapse of Charlemagne's empire, in the face of fierce invasions and fighting among the warlords who were left over from that crumbling political structure. Without a central authority, power devolved upon whatever warrior had enough land, military prowess, and fighting men loyal to him to make his authority felt in a given locality. Such a warlord needed a good deal of land: first to graze his horses, since cavalry was all-important in feudal warfare, and secondly to feed himself, his household, and the men who served him. This meant that numerous small farmers on the lord's land would share what they produced with the lord, in return for his protection. These "serfs" were tied to the land in the sense that they agreed with the lord to remain where they were. Villages grew up on these lands, and serf-craftsmen made most of the materials used on the estates. By the eleventh century, however, the towns had begun to develop, and these were not on feudal estates.

The free towns included merchants and traders who were not part of the feudal system, and they became magnets for other workers—including the serfs, who were supposed to stay on the estates where they were born. It frequently happened, then, that a talented serf—named Odo, perhaps, who had been making shoes for the feudal lord and his vassals—would succumb to the temptation to move to the nearest town and set up his own business there. If his angry lord came storming up to the town demanding that he return, the lord was politely informed that the town had a charter from the new king of the nation, not from a mere local lord, and also that "town air makes free." If a man could support himself in the town for a year and a day, he was considered a free citizen of the town with the right to reside there. As a matter of fact, Odo's year was almost up, since it had taken some time for his absence to come to his lord's attention and for him to be tracked down. Did the lord really want to pursue the case? Unable to storm the walls of the town and unwilling to antagonize the town's royal overlord, the baffled lord would withdraw; thus the rise of towns meant the beginning of the end of the stopgap system of feudalism.

Catholic Monarchy

The above reference to the king recalls another major development of the Middle Ages: the rise of organized nation-states under the central authority of a monarch. Precursors of the great medieval kings had existed during the Dark Ages in the rulers of the Frankish tribe who came to control most of what is now France, Germany, northern Italy, and the Low Countries. One of the most talented and dedicated of these barbarian rulers, Pepin, in the eighth century, was anointed king by the Pope himself—which introduced a concept beyond that of traditional tribal rule. "To us," Pepin declared, "the Lord has given the care of government." No longer was the king a mere warlord, holding his country as his own possession; now he held it in trust, to be cared for by the king for the common good, for which he would answer to God.

Pepin's son was the great Charlemagne, whose reign was seen as a sort of golden age for Europe economically, politically, culturally, and spiritually. It was the fall of Charlemagne's empire that ushered in the two hundred years of invasion, cultural and spiritual decline, local warfare, and economic collapse that produced the institutions of feudalism. By the year 1000, however, the chaos had sufficiently abated for centralized authority to arise once more in the various parts of the former Carolingian empire (Charlemagne's empire), and the great age of the medieval monarchs began.

Here the modern mind shudders. Monarchy, after all, is not democracy, and democracy is the only legitimate system of government in contemporary eyes. Everything else—especially the rule of (horror!) one man—must be bad. Why monarchy, then?

Medieval Political Theory

Medieval thinkers of the twelfth and thirteenth centuries explored the advantages and disadvantages of various systems of government. St. Thomas, writing in response to an inquiry from the king of Cyprus, followed Aristotle in discussing the ideal balance that should exist within a social structure, as well as the stability that is promoted by a sizeable middle class. Like all of his contemporaries (and their ancestors and descendents until the eighteenth-century revolutions), St. Thomas accepted monarchy as a natural, practical, and legitimate form of government. A few centuries later, Robert Bellarmine wrote a little work supporting the idea of republican government. Far from being hauled before the Inquisition for daring to question monarchy, he ended up a canonized saint (for more important things than an academic treatise). The point is that, in contrast both to the Islamic mentality and to today's politically correct (often fanatically so) religion of democracy, the Catholic scholars of the past were nothing if not open-minded. Only if the conclusion of a scholar could be shown to contradict a truth of the Faith did ecclesiastical authority censure it.

From the earliest Christian centuries, monarchy was accepted as reflecting the authority and rule of God Himself. The king was God's representative on earth, as Pope St. Gelasius wrote to the Emperor Anastasius in 494: "Two there are, august Emperor, by which this world is chiefly ruled, the sacred authority of the priesthood and the royal power." He goes on to say that the responsibility of priests is more weighty because they answer to God for souls. On the other hand, in secular affairs the clergy answer to the secular authority, while even kings answer to the Church in spiritual matters. This division between the spheres of Church and State was the perennial principle of the Church in the West. It might (and did) cause occasional friction, but it also produced a creative partnership that proved a hallmark of Western civilization.

Catholic monarchy had a lot going for it. The new nations emerging in Europe, from England to Hungary, needed strong central governments to organize, defend, and stabilize them, as well as to promote economic development, culture, and social welfare. The king was responsible for his people to God; in case of his dereliction of duty, the representatives of the Church called him to order under penalty of spiritual sanctions. In every country there emerged also representative bodies of citizens, whether a single national parliament as in England or the more numerous assemblies found in other countries, to advise the monarch and put forward the needs of the citizens. The kings also protected and assisted the Church in all its works. If there were instances of considerable friction between Church and state, there were many more of cooperation for progress and the common good.

It was in the early stages of the development of national monarchies that alliances between the kings and towns were formed. The kings were still weak; the towns were increasingly powerful in their localities. In return for a charter from the monarch, a town would give him its allegiance and support. The history of the relations between the new, middle-class, urban centers and the new national monarchs is also the history of the development of responsible local self-government with royal sanction, a system that proved so fruitful during the Middle Ages.

It is ridiculous to blame the Church in the ages of Catholic monarchy for failing to criticize the system under which she thrived. Her role was to criticize moral and doctrinal abuses, not to produce abstract critiques of political systems, and in fact Catholic monarchy as a system has a splendid record. The close-mindedness of modern critics, for whom monarchy is synonymous with tyranny or dictatorship and therefore to be condemned out of hand—never mind historical evidence—is another example of how those who trumpet their claims to objectivity most loudly often end up making absolutes of their own judgments.[1]

As for the Church's record in promoting learning and progress in all fields, it is not only unique in history, but it created the civilization of the West. From Clement of Alexandria to Newman, Albertus Magnus to Mendel and Pasteur, Catholic scholars have shaped the modern world. Not a bad record.

---

1 Similarly, modern critics who damn the Church as an obstacle to freedom and progress because she opposes, on moral grounds, evils such as abortion and homosexuality, are simply making absolutes of their own judgments on those issues, thereby claiming an infallibility they deny to the Church.

CHAPTER 3

A CRUSADE AGAINST THE TRUTH

The Lie: The Crusades were medieval crimes against humanity, a prime example of destructive religious zealotry.

I f ever there were a topic apparently tailor-made for historical liars, it is the Crusades. It has all the necessary components of a club with which to beat the Church. Consider the scenario: a pope preaches a sermon calling for armed volunteers to invade a Middle Eastern territory and recover Christian holy places from their Muslim rulers. How politically incorrect can you get?

Anti-Catholics—and the merely ignorant—will see the Crusades in the following way. Fanaticism came first, in the form of a religious mania and superstition that caused a berserk pope to preach a holy war to an unruly mob in 1095, promising them Heaven if they died in battle. Mobs of misguided zealots flooded across Europe and on to Palestine, eager to slaughter the inoffensive people who lived there. Those people were mostly Arabs, but also Seljuk Turks who had recently taken control of the formerly Arab caliphate of Baghdad. The Arabs and Turks were nice, civilized people—very different from the barbarian mobs now slavering for their blood—who were cruelly victimized and murdered by Catholic fanatics. The only offense of these Arabs and Turks was their control of holy places such as Jerusalem, which was a very holy city for them too. They had always been very tolerant of Christian pilgrims, who had been visiting the Holy Land for centuries with no problems; now, suddenly, these guests were turning on their hosts.

The Byzantine emperor, meanwhile, was helpless to control the mass of European Crusaders who were swarming into his capital, so he gave them transport into Asia Minor to keep them from harming his own people. Once there, the crusaders proceeded south in the direction of Jerusalem, slaughtering and pillaging as they went, capturing both Muslim and Christian territories. Finally they reached Jerusalem and attacked it unmercifully: when the army entered the city, the horses were wading in blood up to their knees.

That was the First Crusade. The Turks later retook Jerusalem, provoking a number of subsequent crusader expeditions, equally barbaric and cruel. Obviously the real reasons for the whole enterprise were mercenary and imperialist; in addition to spreading their fanatical religious prejudice, the Christian Westerners intended to conquer as much territory as they could in order to make room for Christian settlers, bankers, and traders. This was the first act in the aggressive imperialism that has been practiced by the West from then until now.

History of Crusade-Bashing

This collection of falsehoods and half-truths goes back a long way. Not surprisingly, post-Reformation England produced a number of historians eager to bash the Catholic Crusades. One was the seventeenth-century scholar Thomas Fuller, who drew up a list of arguments for and against the Crusades. His cons outweigh his pros, though he does raise the issues of the defense of the Eastern Empire[1] and resistance to Muslim aggression. His objections to the Crusades include practical points such as the terrible cost of such wars in both money ("a quicksand to swallow treasure") and lives. He also argues, however, that God might want the Muslims to possess the Holy Lands since He had allowed them to hold them for so long, and he adds that pilgrimages are generally superstitious anyway. In sum, "These reasons have moved the most moderate and refined Papists and all Protestants generally in their judgments to fight against this Holy Warre."

The following century, the eighteenth and the so-called Age of Enlightenment, found anti-Catholic thinkers such as Voltaire, Diderot, and Hume scribbling more attacks on the Crusades. A good example from this period is Edward Gibbon, who wrote about the Crusades with his pen dipped,

---

1 The Eastern (or Byzantine) Empire began in the fourth century when the ancient Roman Empire was divided into two parts, Western and Eastern. The Eastern Empire is known as Byzantium; its capital was Constantinople.

as usual, in anti-Catholic venom. This is the author of *The History of the Decline and Fall of the Roman Empire*, which decline and fall he famously and falsely blamed on Christianity. There are, however, many things in that multi-volume work—which also deals with Byzantine history—that are still useful for historians. What he has to say about the Crusades is not among those things, since diatribe is rarely enlightening. The victory of barbarism, he calls them, stating that "The principle of the crusades was a savage fanaticism. . . . The belief of the Catholics was corrupted by new legends, their practice by new superstitions; and the establishment of the inquisition, the mendicant orders of monks and friars, the last abuse of indulgences, and the final progress of idolatry, flowed from the baleful fountains of the holy war." Obviously Gibbon either had a great imagination or his anti-Catholic obsession clouded his judgment as a historian. Or maybe his brains were getting scrambled after writing seven volumes of the *Decline and Fall* (though he wasn't finished yet).

Despite solid research and positive judgments by modern historians, negative judgments and outright distortions of the facts about the Crusades can be still found throughout the nineteenth and twentieth centuries and into the twenty-first, generally in popular writing and high-school and college textbooks. In a *New York Times* article dated June 20, 1999, columnist Maureen Dowd added the Crusades to her personal list of historical atrocities: "History teaches that when religion is injected into politics—the Crusades, Henry VIII, Salem, Father Coughlin, Hitler, Kosovo—disaster follows." Notice that the Crusades head the list. (She does not say what she thinks Hitler's religion was.) Muslim scholars have explained how much they still resent historical European aggression against them. We also heard a good deal about the Crusades following the attacks of September 11, since according to some the attacks were, at least in part, revenge for those acts of Christian aggression.

Of course it was Europeans who fought the Crusades, not Americans—but never mind, we Americans are guilty too. Former President Clinton said as much in a November 7, 2001 speech at Georgetown University: "Those of us who come from various European lineages are not blameless. Indeed, in the first Crusade, when the Christian soldiers took Jerusalem, they first burned a synagogue with 300 Jews in it, and proceeded to kill every woman and child who was Muslim on the Temple Mount. The contemporaneous descriptions of the event describe soldiers walking on the Temple Mount, a holy place to Christians, with blood running up to their knees. I can tell you that that story is still being told today in the Middle East and we are still paying for it."

The Real Story

All of the above, of course, is hogwash. Unprovoked Muslim aggression in the seventh century brought large parts of the southern Byzantine Empire, including Syria, the Holy Land, and Egypt under Arab rule. Christians who survived the conquests found themselves subject to a special poll tax and discriminated against as an inferior class known as the *dhimmi*. Often their churches were destroyed and other harsh conditions imposed. For centuries their complaints had been reaching Rome, but Europe was having its own Dark Age of massive invasion, and nothing could be done to relieve the plight of the eastern Christians.

An uneasy status quo did prevail for some centuries in the Holy Land, as the Arab empire expanded in other directions, and a number of pilgrims from the West were actually able to travel to Jerusalem and return in one piece. On the other hand, this Arab "toleration" could be wildly unpredictable: as early as the eighth century there are reports of pilgrims being executed, some by crucifixion. By the eleventh century, under the rule of a new Muslim dynasty, conditions worsened. The Church of the Holy Sepulcher, site of the Crucifixion, was destroyed, along with a large number of other churches, and Christian pilgrims were massacred. In 1067 a group of seven thousand peaceful German pilgrims lost two-thirds of their number to Muslim assaults. By this time the popes, including St. Gregory VII, were actively trying to rally support for relief of the eastern Christians, though without success. It was not until the very end of the century, in 1095, that Pope Urban's address at Clermont in France met with a response—though not quite the one he had hoped for.

The First Crusade

So what were the Crusades, really? How can we define this series of military expeditions sprawling over several centuries? An Egyptian-born historian, Aziz Suryal Atiya, has given what seems to be the most fitting description: "The general consensus of opinion among medievalists . . . is that the Crusades were military expeditions organized by the peoples of Western Christendom, notably the Normans and the French, under the leadership of the Roman Popes, for the recovery of the Holy Places from their Muslim masters." This seems to sum up most neatly what the Crusades really were and how their participants actually viewed them. The Crusades were not colonialist or commercial ventures, they were not intended to force Christianity on Jews and Muslims, and they were not the projects of individual warlords. Their primary goal, in addition to the defense of the Eastern Empire, was the recovery of the Holy Land for Christendom, and they acknowledged the leadership of the popes. As French historian Louis Bréhier wrote, "the popes alone understood the menace of Islam's progress for Christian civilization." (There were, however, one or two cases in which papal leadership was flouted or ignored, as we shall see.)

In 1095, then, Pope Urban made a particularly public and urgent plea to Christendom because he had received a letter from Byzantine Emperor Alexis describing the great peril in which his realm had been placed by the increasing power and stepped-up attacks of yet another Muslim tribe, the Seljuk Turks. This group, variously referred to as Turks, Turkmen, Tartars, or Tatars, had moved west from the steppes of Asia. After taking over the weakened caliphate of Baghdad in 1055 they had proceeded to enlarge their empire, at the expense both of other Muslim powers and of Byzantium, and it was they who now controlled the Holy Land. In 1071 the Turks had defeated the Byzantine forces and actually captured the Emperor and forced him to sign a peace treaty, leading to further Turk expansion in Asia Minor. Within a few years the Turks were pushing into Anatolia, also called Asia Minor (roughly equivalent to today's Turkey) and had set up headquarters at Nicaea (site of the famous fourth-century Church council that produced the Nicene Creed), not far from Constantinople (today's Istanbul) itself.

In his famous address, of which a number of versions exist, Pope Urban stressed the need for Western warriors to go to the aid of the Christians of the East, including those in the Holy Land. The idea was to raise an international force of professional soldiers to march to the relief of the Byzantine Empire, but what caught the imagination of masses of people all over Europe was the idea of liberating the Holy Land from the infidel. The idea of a plenary indulgence for "taking the cross"—symbol of a commitment to the Crusade—also appealed to them, though they may have been fuzzy on the conditions required for such a spiritual favor. A knight who took the crusading oath was to do so with a pure intention and sorrow for his sins; if he died while fighting honorably in defense of Christianity, Heaven would be his reward. It is likely that in many cases the spiritual conditions were not met: a mere desire for adventure, loot, or escape from domestic responsibilities (or the law) at home would hardly qualify. However, critics of the Crusades are apt to jeer at the very idea of the Pope's offering the crusaders an indulgence and to assume that he was promising Heaven indiscriminately—like an imam promising jihadist warriors those *houris* and those rivers of wine for blowing themselves up.

The knights of the various nations of Europe began to assemble their weapons and their men, which naturally took considerable time. There were others, however, who did not need time to prepare for travel because they possessed little or nothing. These "others" were many, and they were a significant element in the story of the First Crusade, which held a great appeal for the poor. This is an important angle, well discussed in an article by Walter Porges on non-combatants in the First Crusade. He recalls the long tradition of pilgrimages to the Holy Land and the great growth in the size of such expeditions.

There were eleventh-century German pilgrimages of thousands of people, one of which is mentioned above. In 1064, one such expedition included from seven to twelve thousand pilgrims. The Pope, therefore, must have expected that when the Crusade started there would be many lay people anxious to go along to visit the holy places under the protection of the army. He tried to limit participation by requiring pilgrims to consult their local clergy as to the advisability of making the trip, by discouraging the sick and the weak, and by insisting that even the poor should be willing to fight if necessary. Unfortunately, he was unable to control the great numbers of unsuitable crusaders. Rabble-rousing lay preachers attracted mobs; the sick, elderly, and even children went along in spite of the Pope's admonitions, as did numerous members of the clergy who had no permission to do so. Many of these were in minor orders and may have been eager to leave home because the great Cluniac reform movement was proving too strict for them. Very many of this horde of non-combatants perished before even reaching Constantinople, and many more proved a great burden on the crusading army and the authorized clergy, who had to assist and support them.

Anyway, off they went, but the warriors that Emperor Alexis had requested were not the first to arrive at the gates of Constantinople. The first arrivals were those enthusiastic mobs. With confused notions in their heads of Eastern wealth to be had for the taking, in addition to heroic adventures, they had followed leaders like Peter the Hermit and Walter the Penniless across the continent, looting as they went. They became so dangerous that some rulers closed their borders to them for fear of the damage they would do. Alexis wished he could have done the same when he saw them arrive at his gates, instead of the cavalry and infantry he had been waiting for.

Cold-bloodedly perhaps, though it is hard to think what else he could have done, he had these would-be crusaders ferried across the Dardanelles, where they would get their wish to fight the Turks. They did, and they were massacred. Then came the Crusade of the knights. This was what Alexis had been waiting for. Incidentally the culture shock to a refined Greek upon meeting a group of rough fighting men only a few generations removed from barbarism made a fascinating study for Alexis' daughter, the historian Anna Comnena; it is to her that we owe many of the details of this uneasy meeting. The wealth of Byzantium awed the crusaders—and aroused the cupidity of some of them. Once they had reached the combat zone and begun to liberate imperial holdings from the Turks, some of them were disinclined to return the lands to the Emperor, causing more friction. The result would be small crusader principalities that would survive in Syria and Palestine for two centuries.

The Taking of Jerusalem

The great objective in the hearts of the knights, as it had been for the ill-fated commoners who had perished early on, was Jerusalem. Forgotten was the fact that the holy city had once been part of the Byzantine Empire; it was questionable whether, even if it were restored to the Emperor, he would be able to hold it. The knights were determined to liberate it and hold it themselves. Not forgotten were the atrocities committed by the Turks during their capture of the city some twenty years earlier: although the Seljuk leader had promised to spare the inhabitants, several thousand of them had been murdered as soon as the Turks entered the city. By this time the city was controlled by the Fatimids from Egypt, not the Seljuks, but the warriors from Europe made no distinction between the two Muslim groups, if indeed they were even aware of it.

By the time the multi-national Christian army arrived, divided into contingents with each under its own leader, the men—far fewer than had left home three years earlier—were both exhausted and weakened. They were low on supplies and nearly maddened by thirst under the brutal desert sun in that month of July. Still, they were awed and humbled to be so near the sacred sites where Our Lord had suffered and died for them, and they tried to prepare spiritually to enter the place. Weak though they were, they formed into a procession to walk around the entire circumference of Jerusalem, fasting, singing hymns, and praying.

Here is where the seeds were sown of the brutality the crusaders would exhibit upon entering the city. The Muslim occupiers of Jerusalem, from inside and on top of the walls, kept pace with the Christian army as it moved slowly around the city, jeering at and mocking the soldiers. They went further: they took crucifixes and profaned them in full view of the troops. Horrified, outraged, and nearly maddened at the sacrileges, the armed groups stormed the city furiously. Lack of coordination among the several units of the army made for a chaotic situation, with commanders losing track (and often control) of their men.

Brutal the fighting was, as no doubt it is in any capture of any city in warfare. But were large numbers really slaughtered unmercifully? Did the horses really wade in blood up to their knees and the men up to their ankles? The answer to both questions is, most probably not. The inhabitants had had plenty of time to evacuate the city before the crusaders arrived, and it seems that most of them did. The troops who were left to defend Jerusalem were there to fight, and they did so. Many prisoners were taken for ransom and were released when the ransom was paid, and some commanders took groups of people under their protection and gave them shelter.

Crusader chronicles give varying estimates of how many thousands were slain during the battle. Some of these may be close to the truth, but there also may have been a tendency to exaggerate the heroic achievement of the crusaders by multiplying the number of their adversaries. On the other hand, it is interesting that Muslim sources do not reflect a sense of anything unusual about the siege; it was carried out the way sieges were carried out in those days, and the Turks certainly had enough experience of behaving that way themselves. The magnifying of the capture of Jerusalem into a world-class atrocity for propaganda purposes occurred much later. Now, of course, it is a staple of liberal textbook authors, Muslim writers, and mainstream anti-Catholic writers (not forgetting former-President Clinton). This is not to say that we should not have expected better of the soldiers of Christ that the crusaders professed to be. Especially in that most holy city, they should have exercised both restraint and mercy. Had their leaders—particularly the noble Godfrey de Bouillon—had full control of the troops, had the men not experienced the loss of so many comrades in earlier battles with the Muslims, had their brains and nerves not been affected by hunger and dehydration, the outcome might have been quite different. As it was, the capture of Jerusalem, although a blot on the crusaders' record, hardly vitiates the whole crusading enterprise. Yes, the siege should have been better organized so that the individual commanders had better control of their men, which would have prevented whatever indiscriminate killing of non-combatants took place and also caused less physical damage to the city. We would like it to have been otherwise, but we were not there and we are certainly not obliged to apologize for it: only the guilty themselves can do that, and both they and those who fought the enemy honorably have long since answered to God for their behavior.

After the First Crusade

Within days, once order was restored, captives ransomed, and disrupted urban activity gradually resumed, the crusaders set up the Christian Kingdom of Jerusalem. Their main concern was the protection of the Holy Sepulcher, which they had all longed to visit—and liberate—when they first took their crusader oaths. The clergy argued that the Church should have control of the holy places, including the Holy Sepulcher, but it was also obvious, as the barons pointed out, that the place needed to be defended militarily. By no means all the territory that lay between Constantinople and Jerusalem had been liberated, and attacks could be expected from numerous Turkish strongholds. The upshot was the election, as ruler of Jerusalem, of the most pious, courageous, and honorable of the army's officers, Godfrey de Bouillon. True to his character, he took the job but refused the title of "king," saying—at least according to one source—that he "could not wear a crown of gold in the city where my Savior had worn a crown of thorns." He was therefore given the title of Advocate of the Holy Sepulcher. Almost immediately he had to confront and defeat an Egyptian army, on its way to reinforce the defense of Jerusalem against the crusaders but arriving too late.

In order to fight that battle, Godfrey had to re-call very quickly the numerous crusaders who had already started for home. This is interesting because it shows that they had no intention of staying in the Holy Land and setting up permanent settlements (so much for the crusading enterprise as merely disguised European colonialism). Later on, groups of crusaders would end up staying in the East, but those settlements were not part of any organized imperialism.

The First Crusade was the only successful one; it had helped Emperor Alexis to push back his enemies and put them on the defensive and had recovered Jerusalem for Christianity. Christian possession of Jerusalem and the coastal areas adjoining it would last for nearly a hundred years. It was not until 1187 that the Kurdish warlord Saladin—legendary for his military prowess and chivalric relations with Richard the Lion-Hearted during the Third Crusade—recaptured the city. It was never taken by Christian forces again, though the renegade German emperor Frederick II— "the crusader without faith," Régine Pernoud calls him—was given the keys of the city for a while by a Turkish pal of his in the thirteenth century. Frederick was excommunicated at the time, so he hardly counts as a crusader—but the bizarre saga of Fred the Awful is too complex to get into here.

The Sack of Constantinople

Crusades continued off and on, attacking the Seljuk Turks in various parts of their expanding empire. There is one incident in the Fourth Crusade of 1204 that is frequently cited by critics as an example of Western hypocrisy, brutality, cupidity, etc., just as is the capture of Jerusalem. This was the taking and sacking of Constantinople itself by crusaders in a particularly destructive and brutal siege of that Christian city. (This incident is of course to be distinguished from the sack of Constantinople that took place in 1453.) The version one generally reads is that the crusading army that was supposed to head for the Holy Land, moved by an overpowering greed for the riches of the Eastern capital and possibly also by contempt for the schismatic Byzantines, decided to capture and sack the city and did so with the utmost ferocity—thereby demonstrating once more the real nature of the Crusades.

As with the rest of the anti-Crusade "history," this version relies on ignoring certain facts and distorting others. Definitely, those crusaders who participated in the adventure were blameworthy. They had allowed themselves to get distracted from their goal and pulled into a complex series of political/military schemes that finally led to the tragic sacking. It all started when crusaders got off on the wrong track by attacking an Adriatic seaport that belonged to Hungary. The reason for this was apparently that the crusaders had run up a large debt to the Venetians, who were supposed to transport them. Fewer soldiers showed up than were expected, but the Venetians still wanted to charge for the extra ships. They seem to have proposed that crusader help in capturing the seaport of Zara would settle the matter, and the crusaders agreed, taking the Christian port of a king who had himself signed up for the Crusade. Pope Innocent III strongly condemned the aberration and urged the army on to its real goal. Then, however, a bigger temptation derailed the expedition. A claimant to the Byzantine throne, Alexius, requested crusader and Venetian help in gaining power in Constantinople. In return, he offered to bring the Empire back into union with Rome, help with the Crusade, and pay the remaining money owed to Venice.

Pope Innocent was approached about the plan. He had already refused the proposition when Alexius had made it to him directly, and he rejected it now. So did some of the Crusade's leaders, who then proceeded on their own to the Holy Land. To others, however, it seemed too good a deal to pass up, and so they went to war against Byzantium in order to install Alexius as emperor. Alexius did not find it easy, however, to keep his promise of payment to his Latin allies. They finally gave up on him, and he was killed by his Greek enemies and replaced by an anti-Latin emperor. It was then that the decision to take revenge on Constantinople was made.

The anger that produced a three-day orgy of looting, killing, and destruction was partly based on the long history of antagonism between Latins and Greeks and on the memory of a Byzantine atrocity that had occurred only twenty-two years earlier. In that massacre of 1182, the Greeks had attacked the Latin population of Constantinople and killed men, women, and children, targeting Catholic clergy with particular viciousness. A deacon was decapitated and his head tied to the tail of a dog to show contempt for Rome. According to Archbishop William of Tyre, a contemporary historian, the mob dug up and scattered Catholic corpses, invaded hospitals to kill the sick, and sold thousands into slavery. Now the Latins were taking revenge in the same way; they also profaned holy places and objects, behaving unspeakably. Then they set up a Latin empire; this would endure until it was overthrown by Byzantines in 1261. The Pope got the news in installments. At first he was glad about what sounded like the reunion of the Churches; he was soon horrified when he heard the full story, and he excommunicated the crusaders.

After that disastrous event, crusades continued off and on until the death of St. Louis, king of France, in 1271. He died of disease in North Africa, in the course of his second crusade. With him the zeal for the crusading enterprise died out. It would be partially revived, though with difficulty, in subsequent centuries, as Christendom was faced with invasions of the Ottoman Turks—far more of a threat to Europe itself than the Seljuks had ever been.

Were the Crusades failures, then, since they failed in their goal of permanent liberation of the Holy Land? Louis Bréhier asks this question, and answers it well: "Must one conclude, then, that the Crusades had no historical significance and that they succeeded only in squandering the forces of Europe in a total loss? It is too often forgotten that the Crusade began as a defensive war and that, whatever the inconveniences which may have resulted from it, the Byzantine Empire received from the Crusade an effective protection against the Turks at the end of the eleventh century. . . . If in the fourteenth century Islam resumed its onward march, this happened only after the enthusiasm for the Crusade had died down." It would be this resumed onward march of Islam across Europe itself, into the Italian peninsula and through the Balkans and Austria that would move the popes again to summon Europe to Crusade—although, because of that dying down of enthusiasm, with infinitely greater difficulty.

The Later Crusades

Interestingly enough, although the great military offensives that beat back the formidable onslaught of the Ottomans against Europe were also called "crusades," at least by Catholics, criticism of these seems to be either muted or non-existent. Perhaps the critics rethink their position when Islamic aggression gets close to home—as it certainly did with the sea offensive of the 1570s and the assault on Vienna in 1683, which together could have turned Europe into a Muslim continent sooner than current immigration and demography promise to do. The Ottoman sultans made no secret of their goal of conquering the world for Islam. Whereas states like England, France, and Venice traded peacefully with the Ottoman Empire, that empire was simultaneously pursuing its goal of conquest by attacking Europe repeatedly by land and sea. (One is reminded of Lenin's quip, "The capitalists will sell us the rope with which we will hang them." The Western states were selling ships, raw materials, and anything else their enemies could use—possibly rope too.)

It was the popes and the Church that worked frantically to pierce the apathy of the West in the sixteenth and

seventeenth centuries and to make the nations aware of
their own peril. Several times the call to crusade went out
from Rome; sometimes it failed, with too few answering
the call. Even with the Ottoman fleet en route to the western Mediterranean, the maritime powers dithered; only a
few sent the ships that won the great Battle of Lepanto in
1571. When the Turkish army was approaching Vienna in
1683, the problem was even worse. Even the Holy Roman
Empire, the direct target of the invasion force aimed at
its capital, had trouble pulling itself together to resist the
enemy. The first inclination of the Protestant members of
the Diet (parliament) seems to have been not to support the
war effort. In neighboring Hungary, which was part of the
Holy Roman Empire though then under Turkish occupation, there was even active Protestant support for the Turks.
(In the previous century, Luther had at first welcomed the
approach of the Ottoman army in the first siege of Vienna,
only changing his position as the Turks got really close.)

The Emperor finally won the full support of his Diet
and was able to begin the defense of Vienna, but the same
lack of response was repeated when the Pope called upon
Poland to support the crusade. King Jan Sobieski had to get
the agreement of his Diet also, and that took so long that he
was nearly late for the battle, arriving only in the nick of
time when the Turks were gaining.[2] But the story ends well.
Volunteers had come from all over Europe to the defense of
Vienna, and the failure of the Turks to take it signaled the
beginning of the rollback of Turkish occupation from most
of Eastern Europe.

---

2 See my book *Islam at the Gates*, chapter nine.

How to Defeat the Lie

So what are we to say of the Crusades if we are asked about them? Are we to shuffle our feet and look guilty when moderns attack us for them? Should we agree with Muslim apologists that if only Christians had stayed home and minded their own business they would not now have to worry about jihadis gunning for them? Should Vienna have given Suleiman the Magnificent that "breakfast in Vienna" he had wanted when he besieged the city in 1529; should it have opened its gates to Kara Mustafa in 1683? On what principle can the Crusades of any century be defended? (Note that I am excluding here those numerous expeditions, loosely called "crusades," that were sporadically conducted against heretics or even political enemies of the papacy within Europe. One of these, the Albigensian Crusade, is discussed in the following chapter. The Spanish *Reconquista*, a type of crusade against Moorish Muslim occupation, is addressed in chapter seven. When capitalized, the term "Crusades" generally refers primarily to the wars to liberate the Holy Lands, and by extension to the wars against the Ottoman Turks.)

Beginning with an accurate understanding of the events themselves, freed from lies and distortions, the principle involved in judging the Crusades would seem to be the question of what makes a war a "just war"—a much-discussed topic in medieval Catholic thought. Self-defense against an aggressor certainly justified the use of force—and still does, as all but the most extreme pacifists will agree. This principle would certainly seem to justify the wars against the Turks of the sixteenth and seventeenth centuries. Even when the Christian armies, after having successfully defended Vienna, went on the offensive and pursued the Turks into Hungary and down into the Balkans, they were liberating Christian peoples who had been the victims of Turkish aggression, under which they had suffered for centuries.

What about the justice of the earlier crusades, those directed to the succor of the Eastern Empire and the liberation of the Holy Land? We have seen that the First Crusade occurred in response to the appeal of a Christian emperor for assistance in defending his territory against unlawful aggression. The later ones were necessary in order to defend the liberated Christian territories against repeated attempts by the Seljuk Turks to reconquer them. It is hard to see these responses to aggression as unjust wars.

To recapitulate: the Crusades were a response to unprovoked Muslim aggression against Christian states, as well as a response to the enslavement, killing, and persecution of countless followers of Christ. They were not examples of European colonialism or imperialism, which lay far in the future, nor were they intended to convert anybody; they were a military answer to military attack. The same is true of the later Crusades, those against the Ottoman Turks. Did things happen in the five hundred-year history of the Crusades that should not have happened, or that should have happened otherwise? Of course. Is there any war, however just, of which that is not true? This only proves that human nature is fallible, which—except to utopians—is practically self-evident. To quote Bréhier one last time, "It would be unjust to condemn out of hand these five centuries of heroism which had such fertile results for the history of Europe and which left behind in the consciences of modern peoples a certain ideal of generosity and a taste for sacrifice in behalf of noble causes which the harshest lessons of reality will never erase completely." This concept of generous sacrifice for a noble cause is what led General Eisenhower to entitle his book on World War II *Crusade in Europe.*

Finally, if Catholics need any further reassurance that being pro-Crusade is okay, they can find it in the overwhelmingly favorable opinions of canonized saints. St. Bernard of Clairvaux preached the Second Crusade and wrote the rule for the Knights Templar. St. Louis IX, that royal paragon of holiness and chivalry, died on his second Crusade. Saintly popes such as St. Gregory VII and, later, Pope St. Pius V, called Christendom to Crusade. I cannot think of a saint who ever voiced an unfavorable opinion of these holy wars—just the opposite, in fact. No apologies needed.

CHAPTER 4

THE SINISTER INQUISITION

The Lie: For centuries the Catholic Church sponsored the persecution, torture, and death of thousands, perhaps millions, of innocent people.

Here we should pause for an obligatory shudder at the infamous word which has become a symbol for repression of freedom of speech, freedom of thought, freedom of religion, freedom of the press, freedom to do whatever you want, and all the other "freedoms" so dear to the modern heart: *Inquisition.*

The authorized version of this institution's history says that from its earliest days the Catholic Church has persecuted dissent—starting with Christian heretics and, after the emperors became Christian, hapless pagans in the Roman Empire—by torturing suspects and exterminating the recalcitrant. This continued all through Catholic history: we find the Church hunting down and massacring the easy-going, civilized people of southern France, known as Albigensians, because they dared to have their own ideas on religion. A little later, the infamous Spanish Inquisition would be responsible for millions of deaths, and the subsequent Roman Inquisition of the Counter-Reformation was even crueler, though on a smaller scale. As for the torture and burning of those accused of witchcraft, we have the nauseating testimony of an actual fifteenth-century inquisitor, Heinrich Kramer. This intolerable practice only ceased when enlightened Protestants revolted against the Church and the still more enlightened French revolutionaries started the great movement for human freedom that has spread throughout the world—including to Russia, where the power of the intolerant Russian Orthodox Church was also subdued. Today, finally, we all have freedom of religion and do not have to look over our shoulders in fear of persecution. We can believe anything or nothing, or make up our own religion, without being arrested or burned at the stake. A nineteenth-century historian, whose work provided the foundation for later expositions of the dark and evil history of the Inquisition, exhaustively researched this whole subject. Since the sinister facts are all written down in a book, and by a historian at that, they must be true. (We will return to this historian and to Kramer.)

This highly colored view of the mechanism by which the Church through the ages attempted to protect orthodox teaching comes mainly from the Reformation and

Enlightenment periods (sixteenth and eighteenth centuries). Like the propaganda creation known as the Black Legend, which sometimes overlaps with the Inquisition legends, the "Sinister Inquisition" lie was largely created by anti-Catholic thinkers who were themselves heretics or atheists and who resented measures taken against them by the Church.

In addition to attacking the Catholic authorities who were currently opposing them, these Reformation-era and Enlightenment-era critics went back in history and identified themselves with medieval heretics and any other heterodox thinkers whom the Church had ever dared to sanction. They thus created a powerful myth about free-thinking "real" Christians who had operated outside ecclesial structures for centuries, suffering persecution by the Catholic Church from Roman times until they finally morphed into Protestants in the sixteenth century. This is quite a grand vision, one ably described by Edward Peters in his 1988 work, *Inquisition,* and echoes of it continue to turn up in historical writing and popular literature today. Peters is one of the revisionist historians whom we shall meet later in this discussion whose work has served to demolish the myth and to present the historical reality of the Inquisition.

The Nature of Heresy and the Catholic Response to It

Clear thinking, with all the necessary distinctions, is important to historical truth about the Inquisition because this is not a subject on which our enemies' errors are merely those of fact, such as the number or types of heretics actually killed. The fundamental question at issue is whether a person has the right to think and act upon any and all ideas, no matter how false or morally depraved. The traditional Catholic view, dating from St. Augustine, is that error has no rights. Does that mean that the Church has prosecuted every erroneous opinion about the Faith? Certainly not. Another fundamental Catholic principle is that the free conscience must not be forced. Where forced conversions, for example, have occurred they have always been condemned by the Catholic Church.

Private belief or practice is one thing; attempting to spread a false belief or immoral practice is quite another. In the case of an unbeliever, the perennial practice of the Church has been to spare neither prayers nor pains in attempting to lead him to the truth. The Church did not prosecute an individual merely for his beliefs—a procedure which would hardly attract him to the truth; rather it tried to persuade him that those beliefs were erroneous. It was only when he attempted to proselytize, to convert others to his false religion, or to organize immoral religious practices, that the Church in the Catholic states of Christendom took action to stop this activity—for the sake of both the heretic and his victims.

Catholics have always held that the soul is immeasurably more important than the body. Therefore, one who destroys the faith and grace that are the life of the soul is more guilty than one who merely kills the body. For this reasonable attitude there is surely no reason to apologize. The believers of all religions, until very recently in history, have always considered as absolutely false and pernicious the modern attitude that it does not matter what one believes and that all religions or non-religions are equally good. The traditional principle enunciated by Tertullian and other Church Fathers, and found in Church writing and preaching ever since,[1] is that heresy ought not be allowed to spread, because it destroys souls. Now we can examine this principle as it has been implemented historically in the Catholic Church.

The Early Church and Heresy

There is no question that the first generation of Christians operated on the principles laid down by Our Lord. They were to convert the world by preaching and example, not by force. If one of the converted began to hold false ideas, another Christian was to reason with him in order to make him see his error. If he persisted, representatives of the Church should meet with him. If that failed, they would have to give up on him for the time being and treat him as a non-Christian. In serious cases, this use of the Church's mandate to bind and loose (*Matt.* 16:19) would be in effect excommunication, a parallel to the Jewish casting-out of heretics from the synagogue.

Obviously there is no question here of physical punishment, only of spiritual. In later generations, the early Christians faced more deadly threats, that is, threats from heretics who not only preached false Christian doctrines but often led large numbers of ignorant Catholics out of the Church. What to do about them? Certainly they should not be allowed to destroy the faith within the souls of their victims?

In a few early Christian documents one reads the word

---

1 In the *Summa* (II:II: 11:3), St. Thomas Aquinas famously advocates capital punishment for heretics.

exterminare, which has sometimes been read as "exterminate"—to the glee of those eager to find evidence of Christian bloodthirstiness. Yet what the verb really means in context is to put someone outside the borders (the *termini*) of an area; in other words, to expel or exile him. (If execution is meant, as in later texts, we find the explanatory phrase, "*a mundo exterminare per mortem*" —"to put outside the border of the world through death.") The idea behind exile was to get rid of the source of doctrinal corruption by deporting it. The early Christians had suffered so much sickening torture and persecution themselves that they were not about to inflict it on others, but they were willing to send the troublemaker elsewhere.

This seems to have been generally true, with some exceptions, even after the Roman Empire became Christian. The first Christian emperor, Constantine, permitted religious freedom within his realm. His successors varied in their attitudes towards the paganism that Christianity was gradually supplanting; later emperors began to repudiate their official role in the pagan state religion, to close temples, and even to levy fines on pagan priests. The variation in imperial policy probably stemmed from the difficulty in assessing to what degree paganism had been expunged from the hearts of Romans. The often-cited removal of the beloved pagan statue of Victory from the Senate certainly grieved the pagans, and there were incidents of groups of Christians taking it upon themselves to destroy pagan sacred places and close shrines to false gods. But Christian emperors did nothing to pagans that remotely resembled the persecutions formerly visited upon the Christians, and the principle that *conscience* should not be violated survived even as the *public manifestation* of worship of false gods was sporadically suppressed.

The Case of Arianism

By far the worst of the heresies to emerge within the Roman Empire was Arianism. This collection of heretical ideas can only be called a historical phenomenon, since it went far beyond theological theory: it affected politics, Church-State relations, and historical developments for centuries to come. Henri Daniel-Rops calls it "the great assault [on the Faith] by the mind" and considers it the most formidable heresy in Church history; John Henry Newman produced a classic study of it, *The Arians of the Fourth Century*. We will consider this vast topic briefly here in order to understand better the nature of heresy and the damage it can do.

It all began in Roman Alexandria in the early fourth century when a 60-year-old priest named Arius, an ascetic and scholar whose devoted public loved his eloquent and learned sermons, began to preach a new doctrine. He held that Christ was not divine: Christ was a creature of God, though with divine attributes. The Church, of course, had always taught that Christ is both God and man but had not yet worked out its formulas for defining how that was so. This led to divergent theories, and Arius's became extremely popular, delighting Greek Christian audiences far beyond Alexandria. Early Arianism even appealed to the pagans because of its elegant formulation and its equivocation as to the person of Christ. The controversy raged throughout the empire, with political authorities taking sides and even most of the bishops favoring Arianism at one point.

One man, however, was not seduced; his name was St. Athanasius, and he was only 20 years old when Arius first began preaching his heresy. Athanasius spotted its errors at once and became its sworn opponent, a lifelong champion of orthodoxy even at the risk of his life (he was almost murdered at least once and was exiled several times by Arian-leaning emperors). The Emperor Constantine, on the other hand, couldn't even grasp the magnitude of the issue. "I find the cause is trivial," he driveled in one letter to both Arius and Athanasius. "Basically you think alike . . . the matter between you does not concern an essential point of faith." Fortunately for orthodoxy, the Council of Nicaea that met under Constantine in 325, politely ignoring its patron's foolish remarks, condemned Arianism and issued the Nicene Creed, which stated unambiguously that Christ is "consubstantial" with the Father: that is, Christ is God, as Christians had believed from the beginning. Arians who persisted in their errors were formally excluded from the Church at the Council of Constantinople in 381.

Throughout the Roman Empire during this Arian period, both orthodox clergy and the ordinary faithful had much to suffer. In many places bishops, politicians, and even wishy-washy popes like Liberius accepted Arian—or at least ambiguous—ideas. Some faithful Catholics were forcibly exiled by the Arian authorities, and many others voluntarily accepted the hardship of leaving their native cities when these became Arian, in order to avoid heretical priests. By the end of the fourth century, the Arians were much less of a presence and a problem within the Empire—but only because they had now gone north to preach their heresy to the barbarians across the borders.

Widespread Arianism among many of the barbarian tribes that were to constitute the future states of Europe thus became a headache of a different kind for the Church: it produced a resistance to true conversion among the barbarians and an antipathy to the Roman civilization that the Catholic Church brought with it, and it would lead to wars and other turmoil during the Dark Ages. Nearly all the tribes of Europe adopted Arianism, which became among them a sort of warrior religion with outdoor forest rituals, simple rules, and hostility to Rome. The providential exception among these barbarians was the tribe of the Franks. The Franks remained stubbornly pagan until the conversion to Catholicism that made them the champions of the Catholic Faith and made France the "Eldest Daughter of the Church." It will be largely among the descendents of the Arian tribes that we will find later heresies spreading.

Thus it had become very clear to the Christians of the early centuries that heresy was not a harmless matter of personal opinion; it could and did affect the destiny of nations. Hence it had to be combated whenever it appeared—by attempting to convert the heretics and, in extreme cases, by exiling them in order to prevent further damage to the community of the faithful.

The Medieval Inquisition: Heresy as Treason

The word *inquisition* refers to a court of inquiry into the orthodoxy of religious views professed by individuals or sects. Until the High Middle Ages—the twelfth and thirteenth centuries—such inquiries seem to have been locally organized as the need arose. Since bishops were charged with ensuring the orthodoxy of the Catholics in their own areas, it was their business to investigate heresy. Busy bishops often had little time for such investigations, however, and sometimes they lacked the inclination to get involved in them.

In the early thirteenth century the great Pope Innocent III, although greatly concerned with suppressing heresy and banishing dangerous heretics such as the Cathars, was very lenient toward those of merely *doubtful* orthodoxy. He never mentioned the death penalty, and his policies were a great improvement over the often-cruel local customs of the time.

In a medieval state sometimes secular authority as well as the Church took an interest in investigating heresy, and this for two reasons: first, because both rulers and ruled were Catholic, and any threats to the Faith concerned the whole realm; secondly, because many heretics did not confine their preaching to spiritual matters but advocated *subversive political policies* as well, such as that there should be no temporal authority at all. Often the secular powers were far less gentle than the Church in dealing with heresy.

An early thirteenth-century example of state hostility toward heresy can be seen in the *Constitutions of Melfi,* promulgated in the Kingdom of Sicily by Frederick II, a particularly brutal and unscrupulous ruler. In his statutes for Sicily concerning heresy, Frederick writes, correctly, that "Heretics try to tear the seamless robe of our God . . . they strive to introduce division into the unity of the indivisible faith and to separate the flock from the care of Peter, the shepherd to whom the Good Shepherd entrusted it. Inside they are violent wolves, but they pretend [to have] the tameness of sheep until they can get into the sheepfold of the Lord." Frederick then goes on to attack in similar language one group of heretics, the Patarenes, saying, "We cannot contain our emotions against such men so hostile to God, to themselves, and to mankind. Therefore we draw the sword of righteous vengeance against them." After more of the same uncompromising language, the emperor says that the Patarenes "should be condemned to suffer the death for which they strive. Committed to the judgment of the flames, they should be burned alive in the sight of the people." No one, he goes on to say, should dare to intercede for these people: "But if anyone does, we shall turn against him the deserved stings of our indignation."

There are a number of interesting points about this passage. In the first place, who were these Patarenes? It seems they were originally groups of people in Italy who were particularly zealous for reform at a time when the Church was acting to root out simony (especially the sale of sacred offices) and other immorality. In eleventh-century Florence, a group referred to as the Patarini (probably the same as the Patarenes) had been active in criticizing clerical abuses and immorality. They seem to have had the support of the papacy initially, but later they came to hold that the Orders of—and therefore the Sacraments administered by—immoral priests were invalid. The Patarenes became more militant—and more heterodox—attracting followers mostly from the poorer classes. These Patarenes began to take matters into their own hands and to attack wealthy clergy—who, they claimed, should be living in poverty. When the clergy did not comply, the Patarenes self-righteously looted their houses.

The Paterenes were also said to share the ideas of the

Bogomils, heretics from the Balkans who were somewhat akin to the Cathars. If this were so, it would explain Frederick's mention of "the death for which they strive," since the Cathars condemned matter as evil and sought to free themselves from it by suicide. The tone of the passage reveals the character of Frederick II, who could be cruel, even sadistic, and certainly forceful in suppressing any disorder within his kingdom of Sicily. The burning-alive is a particularly nasty provision; elsewhere, though burning was sometimes employed in the case of notorious heretics, it was often only the corpses of those already executed that were burned, not living persons.

This Fred was no model of Catholic thinking or behavior, and he ended up becoming himself an ambitious heretic who wanted to take over Rome and start his own religion. (He very nearly did it too, but that is another story.) His primary concern was not orthodoxy but maintaining order within what can fairly be called his totalitarian state of Sicily, as well as representing himself to the people as a leader unwilling to tolerate heresy. This blend of religious zeal (or the desire to simulate it) and concern for order within a state or nation was common in the prosecution of heretics, and whether secular or spiritual motives were uppermost was often a moot question.

It is clear that in Sicilian law, heresy was equated with treason. This would be a feature of most heresies during the High and Late Middle Ages. There would no longer be a question of someone being a little bit wrong about the Trinity or about some other purely doctrinal question, but of antisocial groups whose ideas and often behavior undermined the very fabric of a state. Hence the increasing involvement of the state in an issue that in the very early Church would have been dealt with internally.

Pastoral Care and Mercy

By the thirteenth century, the task of confronting heresy had devolved upon the new mendicant religious orders founded by St. Dominic and St. Francis, which were mainly dedicated to preaching the Faith. The aim of these Dominican and Franciscan inquisitors was the *conversion* of the heretic, not his *extermination* (in either of its meanings). There are examples of medieval inquisitors taking long periods of time to explain to an accused man exactly where his error lay, attempting to get him to reject it. The Inquisition was thus the only tribunal in Europe that acquitted a culprit when he repented. That was the inquisitor's primary task, as he saw it: to bring about repentance. He was to bring back the lost sheep, and if he did not succeed in doing so he had failed in his main objective. (In LeRoy Ladurie's *Montaillou,* the classic study of a heretic village by that name and its investigation by inquisitors, we find accounts of the inquisitor sometimes spending days listening to the heretics he was interviewing and trying patiently to lead them to see their errors.)

Punishments for publicly professing heresy, and especially for promulgating it, were generally not severe in the early medieval period; they ranged from making a pilgrimage to undergoing a period of imprisonment. It must be said that in some places, especially where the Cathar sect (a special case, as will be seen below) had aroused the hostility of the local population, there are examples of heretics being rounded up and executed by local secular authorities.

In many other places, however, executions were practically non-existent for centuries, and even imprisonment was mild. There is an example of a prisoner serving his (probably short) term who came down with an illness; his jailors sent him home to recover and told him to come back when he felt better. Another prisoner, who wanted to attend the funeral of a relative, was allowed to do so and asked to return when he could. The system seems almost lackadaisical.

Increased Rigor in Dealing with Heresy

Two things occurred in the thirteenth century that led to more severe penalties. The first was the revival of Roman law by legal scholars, which led to its adoption by the governments of most of the states of Europe. Among the provisions adopted was the use of torture in the interrogation (not the punishment) of suspects. As the practice spread, it began to be used in Church courts also, though not invariably. Even where torture was used in Church inquiries, the rules for it were different from those of secular courts. Torture was only to be administered once in Church courts, as a last resort in obtaining necessary information, and was not to endanger life or limb. This is an important point, because it is often assumed that torture was used *as punishment*— but this was not the case in Catholic courts. In later centuries, particularly in Protestant countries, various forms of torture were used as punishments.

One of the most famous inquisitors, Jacques Fournier (the future Pope Benedict XII), who interviewed some 930 suspected heretics during his career, never used torture; he got all the information he needed through skill and not force. He assigned various penalties to those judged guilty, ranging from making a pilgrimage or wearing a cross to exile or imprisonment. Forty-two heretics he turned over to the secular authority for execution. (The Church itself did not execute; when a crime was judged worthy of death, the criminal was turned over to the state with a request for mercy. Since the crime in most such cases challenged secular authority in some way or was even considered high treason, the request for mercy was usually ignored.)

The second thirteenth-century development that led to increased rigor in dealing with heresy was the formidable threat posed by the Cathar heresy, or Albigensianism, which took strong root in southern France after migrating through the Balkans from western Asia.

The Strange Case of the Albigensians

Of all the heresies in Church history, this was certainly one of the weirdest—and most dangerous. It is often called the Albigensian heresy, from the region in southern France around Albi in which it took temporary hold, but it had existed for centuries under various guises, all of them versions of the same pagan dualism that had probably originated in the Middle East. It was not even a heresy, properly speaking, since that term refers to a false belief that begins within the Catholic Church, and this one did not. Previously known as the Bogomil sect, Albigensianism was active in the Balkans during the Dark Ages, spreading into Italy at the same period under various names.

In the Middle Ages this heresy spread through many parts of mostly southern Europe; it became best known as Catharism, the name of the sect that would take hold in

France. Its teachings were more than bizarre. From its eastern, Manichaean roots it retained a radical dualism: there was a god of good and a god of evil; spirit was good, matter was evil; procreation was evil, so women were suspect (and there were rumors of homosexuality spread about the Cathars). Civil authority could have no claim on a Cathar, so he need not keep any oath or other commitment; his goal was to become so detached from matter that he would become one of the "perfect," starve himself to death, and go wherever good Cathars went. That is, he was *supposed* to starve himself to death, but even one of the "perfect" could be tempted to forget the whole thing if he got hungry enough. Therefore his "friends" would help him persevere in self-starvation by making sure he did not get anything to eat, even if they had to tie him down and sit around him making encouraging comments. (One of the gruesome scenes described in *Montaillou* is the attempted starvation of a baby by Cathar elders—though how a baby could be judged to be one of the "perfect" is unclear. At almost the last minute, the baby's mother could not go through with the murder and snatched back her child to feed it.)

This whole ideology seems so batty, to say the least, that it is very difficult to see how anyone would fall for it. Its success—and indeed it spread like wildfire within some southern French provinces—seems to have been due to a number of external factors. The Cathar missionaries, fanatics through and through, were extremely clever in their appeals. They pointed to examples of clerical immorality, of which there were not a few in the rather lax moral atmosphere of southern France, and to the contrast of those priests' behavior with the seeming uprightness of the Cathar clergy.

They pointed out the grievances of the south in its relations with the French kings: were the southerners not treated as second-class citizens and denied their proper regional autonomy, or even independence? And was not the Catholic Church the ally of those oppressive northern monarchs?

It is probable that relatively few Catholics actually bought the Cathar doctrines, but the appeal to their patriotism resonated with many of them, particularly with the local rulers. A. L. Maycock explains in his *The Inquisition* that the theology of Cathar dualism developed as it grew more popular and entrenched in the south of France, assuming "the form of a definitely anti-social philosophy, aiming at the literal destruction of society." As the situation escalated, Pope Innocent III sent a delegation of friars from the newly formed Dominican Order to look into the situation in the province of Languedoc. One of the legates, St. Dominic himself, dared to reproach a man who was laboring on a feast day (a practice approved by the sect) and was nearly murdered by the populace. In 1207 the fanatics assassinated a senior legate who had excommunicated Count Raymond of Toulouse and placed an interdict on his lands.

The murder brought down more penalties onto the head of Raymond, who was not a Cathar himself, and he soon reconciled himself to the Church. The King of France, meanwhile, had organized the military against the Albigensians: their teachings were not only heretical but were subversive of Christian order and the obedience owed to secular authority. Furthermore, the espousal of the sect by local rulers in southern France had become part of a struggle for independence from the Crown. The northern offensive is known as the Albigensian Crusade, an event that is still raked up as an example of the monarchy's supposed abuse of power in squashing the nice southerners and of the intolerance of the medieval Church and state.

Myths abound about this crusade, which lasted barely two months—and about the whole north-south war, which continued off and on for some twenty years. For instance, the story goes that during one military engagement a papal legate was heard to shout, "Kill them all! God will know His own!" Ludicrous as that sounds, the "quote" has been endlessly repeated as a putative example of Catholic blood-thirstiness. This anecdote is first found in the writing of a chronicler of the siege of the city of Béziers, who puts the words into the mouth of the papal legate. That legate, how-ever, had merely described in his report how negotiations were going on peacefully between the French besiegers and the city authorities when a mob of unruly and unarmed servants and others disobeyed the orders of the command-ers and attacked the city. The situation got out of control, and in the end the city was taken. There is no indication in the papal legate's report of either the words or the attitude attributed to him; the "quote" seems to have originated as a piece of propaganda to be used against the northerners and the Church, propaganda recopied ever since.

It was not until the end of the thirteenth century, in the reign of King Philip the Fair, that Languedoc was brought firmly under the rule of the French crown and France became a truly united country. The Cathars, however, had not yet disappeared; they had merely gone underground. It was only in the early years of the fourteenth century that the surviving elements of Catharism were eliminated from the region, largely due to the efforts of the famous inquisitor

Bernard Gui. He interrogated many hundreds of suspects, of whom 636 were punished: forty with death, three hundred with prison, and the rest with lighter sentences.

Elsewhere in Catholic Europe heresy was also prosecuted, always beginning with attempts to persuade the heretic to retract. Execution seems to have been relatively rare in those countries for which statistics exist. In England between 1401 and 1485, for example, eleven heretics were burned. There may have been others executed for treason: the issue of treason confuses the record everywhere; in some areas little distinction was made between rebellion against the spiritual order and revolt against the temporal order.

The Spanish Inquisition

By far the best known of the various historical inquisitions, and practically synonymous in the popular mind with the term, is the Spanish Inquisition. In part this is the case because the Spanish Inquisition figures so prominently in the anti-Spanish *Black Legend* propaganda that has been produced from the Reformation until now. Yet a recent and welcome revisionism has been taking place with the publication of a number of works based on new research, such as Henry Kamen's *The Spanish Inquisition: A Historical Revision*. The revisionists, using the actual records of the Spanish Inquisition—in many cases for the first time—have helped to demolish long-held myths.

One myth spun by English Protestant writers has to do with the sadistic tortures supposedly used by Spanish inquisitors. It turns out that torture was in fact rarely used, and even when it was, it was very limited. In one group of seven thousand accused persons who came before the Inquisition in Valencia, for example, only two percent were tortured, and for no more than fifteen minutes. Executions were similarly rare. Even the prisons of the Inquisition were a far cry from the dungeons of Inquisition mythology. It was said that prisoners who were going to be tried in the secular courts would often deliberately do something that would get them transferred to the Inquisition so that they would be better treated in jail. It should also be mentioned that appeal from the judgments of Inquisition courts was permitted, and also that those who lodged false accusations were punished. (On the question of appeals, we can recall the trial of Joan of Arc. Utterly illegitimate as was the court that tried her, Joan tried to get it to honor her right of appeal: "I appeal to Rome!" She failed, but the case illustrates the principle of appeal.)

The Spanish Inquisition began under Ferdinand and Isabella in the fifteenth century. It must be remembered that Spain, in becoming a European nation-state, was in a different position from that of its neighbors; Spain had long been occupied by Muslims who had invaded the Iberian Peninsula in the late seventh and eighth centuries. Spanish history from that time until 1492 was essentially the story of the pushing back (and finally out) of these Moorish conquerors. There remained in Spain, however, large numbers of Muslims who still practiced Islam, and numerous other Muslims who had converted to Christianity. There was also a large number of Jews in the Iberian Peninsula, dating back to Roman times. At the time of the Moorish invasions, many of the Jews had welcomed the invaders and cooperated with them, thus earning the hostility of the Spanish.

On the other hand, large numbers of Jews had converted to the Catholic Faith and were playing important roles in both Church and State.

We have then, in Spain at the time of its unification under Ferdinand and Isabella, several distinct groups of inhabitants: the original Catholic Spaniards of Visigothic descent, practicing Muslims, practicing Jews, converted Jews, and converted Muslims. The complicating factor, which became a serious problem as Ferdinand and Isabella struggled both to unite the country and to drive out what remained of the former Moorish rulers, was that some Jewish and Muslim converts were Catholic in name only. For whatever reasons, they had outwardly converted while secretly practicing their original religions and supporting their co-religionists against Spanish unification efforts. They constituted, in effect, a fifth column within the country in wartime. It was at them, rather than at the sort of heretics we have seen elsewhere, that the Spanish Inquisition was primarily aimed. Although the Inquisition was essentially a Church court of inquiry, in Spain it was controlled by the crown, a fact which caused periodic friction with the papacy.

Once unification was achieved and the Moors driven from Granada in 1492, the Inquisition in Spain became less prominent in Spanish affairs. This situation lasted until the Reformation, when Charles V and his son Philip II reactivated the dormant institution in order to keep Protestantism from gaining a foothold in Spain. We should recall that Charles V, before his abdication as King of Spain to his son Phillip II, had been both Spanish King and Holy Roman Emperor. Charles had just come to the throne as a young man in 1519 as Luther was getting going nicely. Within a few years of becoming Emperor, Charles had to cope with the great upheaval of the Peasants' War—which had been incited among the German peasants by some of Luther's ideas, the fighting between Protestants and Catholics within his realm, and the conquest of neighboring Hungary by the Ottoman Turks. Charles was understandably anxious that the appalling disorder and loss of life caused by Protestants in the German lands not spread to his realm of Spain. Thus the Inquisition remained in existence in Spain, keeping on the lookout for Protestant missionaries trying to infiltrate from the north. The very presence of this court seems to have had the desired effect: in the whole of the sixteenth century, the century of the Reformation, the Spanish Inquisition executed one hundred eighty-two heretics, or less than two a year. By comparison, the Protestant persecutions of Catholics in England, Ireland, the Netherlands, and elsewhere in northern Europe, together with the wars of religion, took tens of thousands of lives.

The Roman Inquisition in Italy

During the sixteenth century a tribunal was set up in Rome to deal with the threat of Protestantism in the states of Italy, Malta, and a few other territories. This tribunal also dealt with accusations of witchcraft and with other offenses against orthodox teaching or practice. One of its highest profile cases was that of Galileo, which is discussed in Chapter Five of this book.

The Inquisition in Italy seems to have found very few heretics, at least few who received the death sentence. In the Venetian Republic, for example, from the mid-sixteenth to the mid-seventeenth century, there were four executions out of a thousand cases, with similar single-digit numbers elsewhere in the peninsula. In the course of the Italian Inquisition's nearly two-hundred-year existence, some tens of thousands of cases were investigated, with a small number (estimated by one Italian historian at two percent) ending in a sentence of death. By the mid-nineteenth century its career was largely over, though it continued to be attacked by Italian freethinkers and revolutionaries as a symbol of repression. In the rest of the Italian states, local governments had phased out the Inquisition by the late eighteenth century.

Justice in Non-Catholic Europe

In the rest of Europe during the same period, the sixteenth and seventeenth centuries, punishments for various offenses included such cruelties as disemboweling and gouging out the eyes of an offender. Until the nineteenth century, English law included capital punishment for such crimes as stealing a shilling or chopping down a tree. Indeed, false modern ideas of what supposedly went on in the courts and prisons of the Inquisition would seem to have been drawn from what actually went on in *secular* justice systems—particularly England's, following Henry VIII's break with Rome. For example, the gruesome torture device known as the "Iron Maiden," often attributed to the Spanish Inquisition, was actually a quaint German practice never used by the Spanish. Likewise, the distinction between the use of torture *in inquiry* by Inquisition courts—done only within strict limitations and only for the purpose of obtaining information not otherwise available— is confused with the use of torture *as punishment* by some secular courts, particularly in the north of Europe.

Queen Elizabeth I enjoyed reading the nauseating accounts of her notorious torturer Topcliffe, an expert in inflicting suffering on his victims, particularly Catholics. It was said that during Elizabeth's reign, "the rack was never silent," as the English Catholic martyrs could testify. The charming English custom of hanging, drawing, and quartering a condemned person combined execution with prolonged torture. Horses often drew the victim though the streets to the place of execution, where he was hanged until he was almost—but not quite—dead. Then he was cut down, disemboweled, and his entrails boiled in a kettle before his eyes. Sometimes he was then tied to four horses that set off in different directions, thus pulling apart what was left of him. I know of no account of the Catholic Inquisition that can top that for diabolical cruelty.

The Dark Problem of Witchcraft

The Inquisition was mainly interested in doctrinal errors against the Faith propagated by heretics, not in the superstitious and bizarre practices associated with witchcraft. These had existed long before Christianity, and indeed had posed considerable problems for the early Church in the Roman Empire. Sorcerers with large popular followings would openly compete with Christian preachers—even with saints, in some cases—and sometimes performed greater prodigies than they did. With the conversion of the Empire, the problem of witchcraft and other diabolical activity greatly diminished, but missionaries to the pagan tribes in northern Europe encountered it there.

An interesting—and creepy—phenomenon is the great

resemblance between manifestations of the occult that were widely separated geographically and chronologically. The practitioners of various spells and other kinds of "magic" in places separated by thousands of miles and a couple of centuries are found to be doing almost exactly the same things, and yet they could have had no possible contact with each other. This lack of variety in manifestations despite wide separation argues both for a common source, Satan, and for that dark angel's peculiar lack of originality.

By the time the conversion of Europe had been achieved, occult practices had retreated to the margins of life, and there was a healthy skepticism about the very existence of witches. One early medieval king, possibly St. Alfred the Great, rejected the suggestion that he investigate the activity of witches with the explanation, *"Quia non sunt"*— "Because there aren't any." As for the Inquisition, it was forbidden in the thirteenth century from bothering with witchcraft cases because its focus was to be doctrinal heresy, not superstition and black magic. This attitude prevailed during the Ages of Faith but had changed by the fifteenth century, when cases of heresy mixed up with the occult began to turn up. In many cases, such investigations were the result of popular complaints about such activities.

In the sixteenth century, the famous witchcraft hysteria gripped northern Europe, mostly in Protestant areas. It seems to have arisen partly from the obsession of Protestants, such as Luther, with the devil. (By the eighteenth century, many Protestant sects had gone the other way, removing references to the devil from their catechisms and rites.) From the earlier period arise many of the lurid accounts of torture and burning that are wrongly associated with the Inquisition, since the cases that actually occurred were mostly affairs of local courts influenced by popular hysteria—and in any case, the Inquisition did not operate in Protestant areas! Where it did still operate, in Spain and Italy, charges of witchcraft were mostly dismissed or resulted in mild penalties and few executions.

Statistical data and accurate information are hard to come by concerning the Inquisition in the Reformation and post-Reformation period. The picture is complicated by historians' long reliance on tainted or fictional sources. The widely cited *Malleus Maleficarum,* for instance, is a lurid account of investigations of witchcraft by an inquisitor, Heinrich Kramer, who was censured and fired as inquisitor within a few years of writing the book. The supposed papal approbation for the book is in question, and there is evidence that even during his brief career in the courtroom Kramer was reprimanded by judges for his methods. The work is still excerpted in collections of primary sources used in colleges, but it can hardly be considered reliable. Another source widely used by writers was a nineteenth-century French history of the Inquisition by a forger of evidence named Etienne Léon de Lamothe-Langon. His detailed accounts of witch trials and large numbers of executions were accepted at face value and quoted by historians until the 1970s. That is when historian Norman Cohn smelled a rat and began to investigate both Lamothe-Langon's scholarly credentials and his facts, neither of which turned out to exist. Other supposed historical accounts were also examined and exposed in that same decade. The moral is this: take anything on witchcraft written before the 1970s with a large grain of salt.

The newest estimates are that most executions for witch-craft, by local, secular courts, not ecclesiastical ones, occurred in Germany and Switzerland and numbered per-haps twenty thousand. (In Ireland, the figure seems to have been exactly four.) Ironically, at the time of the Salem witch trials in Massachusetts, a woman who was summoned before the Inquisition court in Mexico on a charge of witch-craft brought by some priests (possibly at the request of her neighbors) was completely exonerated and the priests were reprimanded for being gullible and acting unjustly. The Salem "witches" were not so fortunate as to be investigated by the Inquisition.

Benefits of the Inquisition

We have seen that the original goal of the Inquisition was to protect the purity of the Faith in the souls of the faithful. It should be obvious that there is no obligation to "tolerate" errors in doctrine that can endanger the supernatural life of the soul. The destruction of that life was always considered a greater evil than the murder of the body. Therefore, her-etics who would destroy the souls of others had either to be converted or prevented from doing harm through exile— or, later on, by other punishments, which could include the death penalty.

The political motives that were mixed with religious movements such as Catharism, as well as the difficult prob-lem of false converts in Spain, often meant that the role of the State in dealing with heresy was greater than that of the Church—and also that the Church was able to exercise little control over the methods used, as was at times the case in Spain. There can be little doubt, however, that in most periods the various inquisitions did work for the good of souls. The sinister dualism of the Cathars would certainly have triumphed in a large area of France without the persistent efforts of the inquisitors, quite apart from the armed expeditions of the French kings. (Even Henry Charles Lea, the fierce critic of inquisitions in general, admitted that in the case of the Cathars, the Church was on the side of the angels.)

Similarly, the preservation of Spanish Catholicism, particularly from the Protestant infiltration that would have brought the civil wars and other disasters it had already caused in the north, was surely to the credit of the Inquisition. Were there cruel inquisitors in some places? Of course. Were methods of interrogation distasteful to modern sensibilities? Sure—though we can certainly think of worse methods employed even in our enlightened modern times. Given its formidable task of guarding the purity of the Faith in Christian souls, however, the overall record of the Inquisition in dealing with heresy is not only defensible but admirable.

CHAPTER 5

SCIENCE ON TRIAL:
THE CATHOLIC CHURCH V. GALILEO

The Lie: The Church has routinely suppressed science and per-secuted scientists, proving that its religious doctrines are incom-patible with reason and empirical knowledge.

W e all know the authorized version of the Galileo story. Using a telescope that he invented, this brilliant astronomer discovered that the earth goes around the sun. The Catholic Church, hostile to science as always, opposed him because of biblical passages about the immobility of the earth. Hauled before the dreaded Inquisition, Galileo would not deny his findings and was therefore arrested, tor-tured, and humiliated. Before a mob in a packed auditorium he was badgered and threatened until he confessed that his ideas were false and was sentenced to prison. He tottered out of the courtroom a broken man, yet still defiantly muttering, *"Eppur, si muove"* ("And yet it does move"). Until recently, this was the view of the Galileo case found everywhere in textbooks and works of popular history. For example, Jackson Spielvogel, author of a history text widely used in college courses, refers to Galileo's summons before "the dreaded Inquisition," and a film on the history of science that used to be shown at one of the Smithsonian museums in Washington, D.C. included a dramatized scene of the "trial" complete with packed courtroom and a cowering scientist.

What is most interesting about the legend, which has been the subject of ingenious variations as well as of fanciful paintings, drawings, and literary productions, is that it was not created until the 1760s, over a century after Galileo's death in 1642. The late eighteenth century was the heyday of the Enlightenment, with *philosophes* in several countries looking for any and all clubs with which to beat the Catholic Church: "the infamous thing," as Voltaire called it. The Galileo legend was intended to discredit the Church, bring the supposed evils of the Inquisition back to public attention, and demonstrate how anti-science and anti-progress religion had always been.

It seems that a new religion had emerged, palatable to agnostic intellectuals beginning with the Enlightenment: the religion of science. This new religion had its foundational doctrine—nature and science were henceforth to be the measure of all things, the standard for all human institutions—and a convenient theology called Deism. The

Deist god had created the world and set things in motion, but thereafter, most conveniently, did not concern himself with them and placed no obligations on his creatures. He served as a convenient first cause until more modern scientists came to feel no need for him. The new religion had its myths, and one of them told of the persecution of heroic scientists by unenlightened enemies. Chief among these myths was that of Galileo's travails at the hands of the ancient enemy of progress, the Church. We will watch the development of this new and militant religion of science, or scientism.

The Church, Science, and Heliocentrism

In Chapter Two we considered the role of the medieval Church in fostering science and progress. Here we will consider first the history of the heliocentric theory and the attitude of the early modern Church toward science and scientists, and then the facts about what has become one of the most famous, and infamous, court cases in history.

The main issue at stake in the drama of Galileo Galilei was what goes on in the heavens—whether the earth, the sun, and the planets move around a stationary earth, or whether the earth itself moves. To us the topic hardly seems to be of such vital importance as to spark a furious controversy (that has not yet subsided). Certainly it never had before the sixteenth century, but in that era of discovery, natural science—including astronomy—had become the passion (or the hobby) of a great many intellectuals, including monks, cardinals, and popes.

Galileo was not the first to think about the heavens. Ancient Greek astronomers had developed a number of theories about celestial motion. Ptolemy, Aristotle, and others espoused versions of the geocentric theory, which posited the earth as the fixed center around which the other bodies in our solar system moved. Ptolemy's version proved to be so accurate in accounting for the positions of the stars at all times that it is still useful for navigational purposes: it was a theory that worked. The first known advocate of the heliocentric theory—the idea that the sun is the center of our planetary system—was Aristarchus in the third century B.C. His novel system, however, did not meet with acceptance in the Greek world. It did not work for practical purposes as well as Ptolemy's theory, and it lacked the perfectly circular orbits with immobile centers that Greek thought preferred.

Some medieval thinkers seem to have been dissatisfied with the systems of Ptolemy and Aristotle, and there may be a hint of this in St. Thomas Aquinas's remark, quoted in Chapter Two above, that we are not obliged to believe the theories of the astronomers because there could well be some other explanation for the movements of the heavenly bodies. The late medieval physicists, such as Jean Buridan, on whose work Newton seems to have built, may have had the same reservations.

It was not until the time of Copernicus, in the early sixteenth century, that the heliocentric theory was again taken up and elaborated in a published work. Nicholas Copernicus was a Polish cleric, a cathedral canon involved in ecclesiastical administration, as well as a professor trained in law and medicine. His theory posited that the sun, not the earth, was the center of the universe. Copernicus and his religious superiors were aware that certain biblical references to the heavens seem predicated upon the immobility of the earth and the motion of the sun and stars around the earth. It was a delicate thing to espouse a scientific theory that could be seen as contradicting Scripture; however, it was also commonly accepted that much of Scripture has other meanings than the strictly literal.

One of Copernicus's most virulent critics was Martin Luther, who did not mince words in his criticisms of a great many things. Calling Copernicus "a fool," Luther noted that in the Bible Joshua had "commanded the sun to stand still and not the earth." Other critics objected that the earth could not move through space as fast as Copernicus said it did, because of its weight, and that if the earth were spinning it should cause dropped objects to fall behind, instead of directly below, the point from which they were dropped. They questioned how the moon could orbit both the earth and the sun at the same time, and they wondered why things did not simply fall off a moving earth. These were not stupid questions, and some of them would only be answerable in the following century when Newton analyzed the concept of gravity and applied it to astronomy. Meanwhile Johannes Kepler, building on the observations of Tycho Brahe, would refine Copernican theory to make it more plausible (this so aroused the ire of Protestants at the University of Tubingen that Kepler had to flee to the Jesuits for protection in 1596).

By the time of Galileo in the early seventeenth century, natural science had become almost a fad for scholars and intellectuals. Everyone from the teaching Jesuits to the Pope to members of the curia seemed to dabble in it, especially in astronomy. Both clerical and secular scholars were fascinated by new scientific discoveries, and it is worth repeating here that those sciences had flourished in the West throughout the Middle Ages and into the age of Copernicus and Kepler with the encouragement and patronage of the Catholic Church. Enter Galileo.

A Tale of Two Florentines

Pope Urban VIII and Galileo were both from Florence, both educated men interested in astronomy, and both possessed of strong characters and healthy tempers. Galileo, in particular, was anything but tactful when he thought he was right about something, and he could be pigheaded when someone tried to correct him (as his friend Pope Urban tried to do about the motion of the tides). Scholars have pointed out that Galileo did not discover sunspots (Fabricius did), that he did not invent but merely improved the telescope, and that his notion that comets were optical illusions was nonsense. Most recently, scholars have become interested in exhuming Galileo's remains to try to figure out how bad his recurring eye problems really were, and how much they were responsible for some of the howlers Galileo came up with, such as his theory about the shape of Saturn and his notion that Saturn's rings were moons.

In fact, Galileo seemed to thrive on controversy on a wide range of questions. When he began to champion the Copernican theory as a fact, he was met not only with scientific skepticism but also with the problem of those scriptural passages that appeared to contradict the theory. Convinced as usual that he was absolutely right, and impatient with the skeptics, Galileo went to Rome to try to obtain support and patronage from the highly placed in both society and the Church, including from his papal admirer. His public trumpeting of heliocentrism, however, upset pastors of souls, who feared that their flocks' faith in the Bible might be disturbed. The Pope tried to persuade his headstrong friend to espouse Copernicus's idea as the mere theory it was; although the Bible was not intended to teach science, it would be necessary to avoid the appearance of contradicting Scripture. (It is also possible, according to some sources, that the papacy—still anxious to heal the Protestant rupture—was concerned with not appearing to support an idea that scandalized the Lutherans and Calvinists.) Another issue was the fact that Galileo's version of heavenly motion included details, such as perfect circular motion for the planets, which failed to satisfy other astronomers on technical grounds. Furthermore, Tycho Brahe's theory had not been disproved; perhaps it would turn out to be closer to the truth than the Florentine's.

Galileo, however, seemed to have little sensitivity to the delicacy of the issue, and he went on the offensive in two disastrous ways. He himself related in a letter how he had dealt with the controversy at a dinner party in a fashionable house. "I commenced," he boasted, "to play the theologian." Were his enemies using Scripture against him? *He* could interpret Scripture too, and he would demonstrate that in fact Scripture supported *him* and not his opponents. Thus Galileo claimed the right to decide what Scripture means in the light of his unproven theory—which is not so far from the Protestant practice of private interpretation. He went further, publishing a fictional dialogue between characters espousing his own views and a fool ("Simplicio") who supports Aristotle, going so far as to put the words of

Pope Urban into the fool's mouth. Galileo had gratuitously given his opponents more than enough ammunition for a procedure against him.

The Legendary Trial

"There was only one trial of Galileo," writes Dava Sobel in *Galileo's Daughter,* "and yet it seems there were a thousand." That brief episode in 1633 has become both legendary and infamous. Many years had passed since the Florentine firebrand had created such a stir with his insistence on the absolute truth of his theory. In the interim, the bubonic plague had returned to Italy, causing many to die, others to fall desperately ill but recover, and others to flee their homes for uncontaminated areas. The Thirty Years' War—a devastating international conflict that was in many ways an ominous foreshadowing of World War I—raged from 1618 to 1648, preoccupying the papacy as well as the rest of Europe. Still, attempts had been made since 1616 to find a formula to settle the standoff with Galileo that was dragging on and on.

St. Robert Bellarmine, cardinal and a friend of Galileo's, had made it clear that since the astronomer's theory had not been proven to be true, it must be held only as a theory. "I say," he wrote, "that if there were a true demonstration that the sun is at the center of the world and the earth in the third heaven, and that the sun does not circle the earth but the earth circles the sun, then one would have to proceed with great care in explaining the scriptures that appear contrary, and say rather that we do not understand them than that what is demonstrated is false. But I will not believe that there is such a demonstration, until it is shown to me." It goes without saying that it was never shown to him because Galileo really had no proof. (Opinion varies as to when—if ever—the heliocentric theory was satisfactorily demonstrated. Various nineteenth-century discoveries are usually mentioned as probative, though whether the subsequent theory of relativity affects the claimed proofs I have no idea. To this non-scientist, it is also puzzling that the geocentric theory is apparently still useful for navigation, including space navigation.)

By the time the "trial" occurred, Galileo was in his seventies and not in the best of health. He was never tortured or in fear of torture. He was never truly imprisoned; while in Rome he lived first in the Florentine embassy and then in an apartment in a Vatican palace, with a servant. His food and wine were provided by the embassy. There was no huge courtroom full of enemies of the accused; those present were Galileo, two officials, and a secretary. The report of the officials was then submitted to a tribunal of ten cardinals, of whom three refused to vote on it.

Why did the Church go to such lengths to obtain a retraction from Galileo? There were a number of reasons, some of them weightier than others. No doubt the public mockery of the Pope, in the *Dialogue* that Galileo had published in 1632, had displeased Urban, especially since its author had been warned repeatedly since 1616 to stop teaching his theory as a fact—and yet there he was coming out with still another justification for it. More important reasons for silencing him included those touched on above: upsetting the beliefs of simple people who were disturbed at the notion that the truths of the Bible had somehow been disproved by science; the harm done to attempts at reconciliation with the Protestants by the impression given by Galileo that Catholics did not accept biblical truths; the blanket discrediting of scientific and philosophical authorities such as Aristotle, whose thought contained much that was valuable for Christian scholarship; the possibility that there existed some alternative theory that might be consistent with the same astronomical facts. On the last point, Arthur Koestler in *The Sleepwalkers* has remarked that since Galileo's theory included erroneous details and in any case had certainly not been proven, if Galileo had succeeded in mobilizing ecclesiastical authority in his favor, the Church would then have been attacked for its gullibility. Paul Feyerabend rightly notes that "the Church in Galileo's time adhered to reason much more than [did] Galileo himself."

In any case, Galileo did sign a retraction and was sentenced to imprisonment, though it was a foregone conclusion that due to his age and health the imprisonment would really be a sort of house arrest: he was to go home to Tuscany and stay there. Descartes pointed out that this was merely the disciplinary action of a committee, not confirmed by the Pope. In his comfortable house Galileo spent the ten peaceful years before his death producing what is probably his best work: one on physics, not astronomy. He seems to have been a much better physicist than astronomer, and Newton used his work on motion and gravity. Finally, Galileo did not say "And yet it does move" as he left the courtroom. There is no contemporary record of his saying this; the claim first appears in a book about Galileo written over a century later.[1]

---

1 It is possible that Galileo did utter these words and that the account thereof was

After the Trial, the Legend

The lie asserts that the Church continued to persecute that poor old man even after his death: that his books were suppressed, his reputation continued to be blackened, and the vindictive papacy never came to terms with his great discovery—and that all of this demonstrates the irreconcilable hostility between science and religion, as well as the permanent close-mindedness of the power structure of the Catholic Church and of the Inquisition.

Of course none of this is true either. In the century following the trial, Pope Benedict XIV approved the publication of a complete edition of Galileo's works, granting them the Imprimatur. And today we certainly have no call to apologize for the censure of Galileo. The many years that passed between the time when he first burst onto the Roman scene and his "trial" were spent in long dialogues between other astronomers and Galileo, between the Pope and Galileo, and between Cardinal Bellarmine and Galileo. These oral and written conversations were generally conducted, at least on the side of the astronomers and clergy, reasonably and moderately. We seem to find all the bluster, sarcasm, and extravagant claims on Galileo's side. It is easy to see how he would get on the nerves of his critics, especially with his gift for ridicule. Given the very human emotions of

---

somehow passed on by word of mouth for over a century until it got recorded, but we have no evidence for that either. I can imagine Galileo, back in Tuscany, regaling his friends with an account of his adventures: "And so I stalked out, saying defiantly, 'And yet it does move!'" "Did you really say that out loud, Gally?" "Well, I may have lowered my voice a little; I didn't want them to call me back because I was due at a banquet at the embassy." "But we can quote you, can't we, Gally?" "Well, er, yes, of course . . . it's what I still say now. Those Romans are so obtuse they can't even understand that comets are just optical illusions."

exasperation that he aroused in the targets of his mockery, it is perhaps surprising that he got off with a figurative slap on the wrist. One may also wonder if that excellent work on physics would ever have been completed had he been free to keep on promoting his version of heliocentrism. It would indeed be ironic if the "'trial" were actually responsible for Galileo's best contribution to science.

Galileo Today

The issue simply will not go away. An online article, *God and Science: An Inner Conflict*, dated January 15, 2009[2] analyzed the question of whether there is an inherent opposition in our brains between the concept of God and the teachings of science. It seems that a recent study which monitored the automatic reactions of test subjects to subliminal exposure to the words "God" and "science" concluded that the human brain is incapable of holding simultaneously two such contradictory concepts; supposedly we can only believe in one of them at a time. The study has been criticized, with one historian suggesting that if people appear to find God and science incompatible, this it is not because of an inherent opposition in the brain but because we have been conditioned by our culture to *think* there is such a conflict. One of the researchers agreed but argued that this appearance of a God-vs-Science contradiction has become part of our "knowledge structure," since the nineteenth-century publication of writings citing—guess what?—the Galileo case.

Naturally the article gets it wrong, stating that the Church

---

2 http://www.livescience.com/culture/090115-god-science.html

taught that the earth was the center of the universe (it did not), then saying nice things about Galileo and noting that he has been "mostly redeemed," whatever that may mean. There is no mention of the fact that Galileo was unable to prove his dogmatic statements, or that if the Church had endorsed an unproven theory which turned out to be wrong it would certainly have been blamed for that. A recent news story about the ongoing research on Galileo's eyesight referred to the "stress" on Galileo caused by being put on trial because the Copernican theory contradicted the Bible—as if the Church were really responsible for his worsening eyesight and therefore his errors in astronomical observation. Of course the problem was not the Copernican *theory*, which Copernicus himself was allowed to publish with ecclesiastical approval, but Galileo's insistence that it had been proven, and that he was the man who had proved it.

Cui Bono?

What good does it do for the Galileo case to be resurrected and publicized every few years? Who profits? Of course the authors of books about the necessary opposition between science and religion profit, since they are usually big names, and what they write sells many copies. Those who know the truth write books and articles too, but the tide is not with them and their sales are always modest. A number of the recent works on dear old Galileo and how he was persecuted by the Inquisition are written for young people, who will thus have their brains conditioned to think science: good, religion: bad at an early age. Besides the book writers and booksellers, the enemies of the Church and the worshippers of science certainly have a stake in keeping simple-minded and slanted accounts of the case before the public: they have been doing so since the Enlightenment.

It certainly did not help that a recent pope publicly apologized for the Church's treatment of Galileo.[3] In 1979, near the beginning of his pontificate, Pope John Paul II ordered a review of the Galileo affair. A commission composed of several sections was set up, headed by Cardinal Poupard, who recommended that the Church own up to how it had wronged Galileo. The Pope, however, seems to have accurately noted Galileo's original error of presenting as fact what was only hypothesis. At the ceremony of rehabilitation, apology, or whatever we want to call it, the Pope recalled that Galileo had long been rehabilitated already by virtue of the *Imprimatur* on his works. (We might ask: in that case, why do it all over again?) The Pope explained that "the underlying problems of this case touch both the nature of science and the nature of the message of faith. It cannot be ruled out, then, that we might find ourselves in a similar situation one day and that it will demand of one side and the other a knowledgeable awareness of the scope and the limits of their respective fields." It seems to this historian that the committee that tried Galileo was quite aware of that scope and those limits, which were the very reason for the trial. It was Galileo who would not accept them. In any case, this noncommittal statement by the Pope was trumpeted in media throughout the world as an apology that admitted the Church's "error" in condemning Galileo.

One important tactic now being used to attack the Church

---

3 A learned priest who was speaking to one of my classes commented, "I hear the Pope has apologized for the Galileo case. I want to apologize for the Pope's apologizing."

on scientific grounds, thereby reinforcing the lie that religion and science are incompatible, is the redefining of moral or dogmatic issues as being merely "scientific," thus making the Church's stances on them "anti-science." Consequently, the Church's opposition to abortion is deemed hostility to women's health, which of course is a matter of medical science. The Church's opposition to contraception and homosexuality allegedly shows an obdurate opposition to the scientific conclusions of specialists in human physiology, psychology, biology, and once again, "health." We Catholics are "unscientific" again in our rejection of in-vitro fertilization and embryonic stem cell research, human cloning, and euthanasia for the terminally ill. For its most zealous adherents, science—or scientism—is the only rational religion, a religion in which scientists are the high priests, and in whose eyes Catholics are the worst of heretics. Galileo got off much easier than we do in the judgments of the inquisitors of science.

The Real Target: God

The target for many of those high priests, however, is no longer merely the Church itself and the way it handled one court case. Since the eighteenth century, God Himself has come under attack in the name of modern science and its mechanistic universe. As Carl L. Becker wrote in *The Heavenly City of the Eighteenth-Century Philosophers,* "Obviously the disciples of the Newtonian philosophy had not ceased to worship. They had only given another form and a new name to the object of worship. Having denatured God, they deified nature." In the nineteenth century we see Darwin arguing against God in his writings, with surprising persistence. Cornelius Hunter has documented the struggle in his *Darwin's God and the Problem of Evil,* noting how many times Darwin insists that "God would not have done it that way" when he comes across some development in nature that does not square with his idea of a sort of tidy Victorian deity who would not tolerate the waste and inefficiency Darwin observed in the natural world. The more he elaborated his theory of blind evolution to account for the origin and development of things, the harder it was for him to preserve his faith in a God that did not fit the theory. Exactly what Darwin believed at the end of his days is unclear.

Today's neo-Darwinists are still oddly preoccupied with God and always seeking ways to discredit Him. In a 2002 interview on National Public Radio, the late biologist and celebrated atheist Stephen Jay Gould was asked about a recent discovery in astronomy. After describing the discovery, the interviewer asked Gould what it meant. The question was a natural query, but Gould's reply was extraordinary. What the discovery meant, he answered, was that God was either incompetent, an idiot, or nonexistent. This was a gratuitous sneer that had nothing to do with science and everything to do with Gould's obsession with God. Three weeks later Gould was dead; presumably he knows the answer now.

For the new atheistic scientists, the Galileo case is still alive, as David Berlinski notes in his excellent book, *The Devil's Delusion: Atheism and its Scientific Pretensions*: "Far more than Isaac Newton—implacable, remote, incomprehensible in his genius—Galileo Galilei has entered contemporary life as the very soul and symbol of a way of thought." Berlinski also points out, however, that science has moved on: "The long Galilean moment in the history of thought is coming to an end."

Enduring Results

To return to the famous case: the Church was right in requiring more proof than the mere assertions of Galileo, and Galileo was wrong in trying to make a hypothesis into a fact. What are the enduring results of the Galileo case? Partly because of Galileo, our brains are now presumed to be hard-wired to posit an opposition between science and the God that created it. Also, many modern scientists seem obsessed with discrediting any connection between God and His creation. Galileo would not have liked that at all.

CHAPTER 6

A CHURCH CORRUPTED TO THE CORE

The Lie: The Protestant Reformation was necessary, since the Catholic Church had become utterly corrupted by immorality and false doctrine.

As is the case with all the other historical lies, there are numerous examples of exhaustive research by both Catholic and non-Catholic scholars that disprove this one. The problem is that careful scholarly research, backed up by a multitude of footnotes in fine print, does not attract the very readers who should know about it. There are, however, a number of works on the topic—by both Protestants and Catholics—which are readable and which succeed in presenting a balanced picture. Some will be mentioned in this chapter, while others will be included in the sources described in Appendix 2.

Here's the authorized popular version of this lie in a nutshell: the Reformation was unavoidable. (Even Catholic art historian Sir Kenneth Clark, in his *Civilisation* film series, says, "It had to come.") By the sixteenth century things were so intolerably bad in the Catholic Church that somebody just had to do something. Fortunately, benefactors of mankind like Martin Luther, John Calvin, and Henry the VIII arrived to take up the job of purifying Christianity, which had been corrupted by centuries of Catholic greed and superstition.

The Catholic clergy were morally corrupt as well as ignorant; they lived in concubinage or worse, and they sold pardons for sins (see the character of the Pardoner in Chaucer's *Canterbury Tales*). The monasteries were cesspools of iniquity. At the higher levels, clerics bought and sold their offices and their political and ecclesiastical influence. The popes lived immoral lives in great luxury, concerned mainly with political affairs, like the worldly princes they were. The laity were ignorant wretches, bled dry by the tithes and taxes imposed on them by the clergy and filled with superstitions taught to them under the guise of doctrine. They could hardly function as rational human beings because of their preoccupation with relics, the afterlife, and arcane practices such as the Mass.

It was in matters of doctrine, in fact, that the corruption of the Church was most obvious and glaring. Not only did the lives of the clergy resemble those of the Apostles in absolutely nothing, but what they taught had no basis in Scripture. Indulgences, for instance, are certainly not in the

Bible, yet they were a major source of income for the corrupt clergy. The Catholic Church as a whole, with its mysterious liturgy, magical Sacraments, and many incomprehensible doctrines, bore absolutely no resemblance to the simple Christian communities we find in the Bible. Since, then, the Catholic Church was obviously incapable of reforming itself—the so-called reforming council that was held in the early sixteenth century (Fifth Lateran Council) accomplished absolutely nothing—it was time for a radical shake-up and thorough cleansing by devout Christians who knew what Christianity was all about.

This is the Protestant story of the great Reformation. As a French Protestant historian, E. G. Léonard, wrote, ". . . the Protestants long maintained, and still do occasionally, that the Reformation was a reaction against the licentiousness of the priests and the debaucheries of the Papacy; they are confirmed in this view by a late writing in which Luther claims that his revolt arose from his horrified discovery of the shameful practices of Rome, during his visit to Italy." (In *The Reformation: Revival or Revolution,* edited by W. Stanford Reid.) Will Durant, in the Reformation volume of his *The Story of Civilization,* takes the opportunity to paint a lurid picture of widespread clerical corruption and then adds, maliciously and cleverly, "In fairness to these lusty priests we should consider that sacerdotal concubinage was not profligacy, but an almost universal rebellion against the rule of celibacy that had been imposed upon an unwilling clergy by Pope Gregory VII." Celibacy he calls "an arbitrary rule unknown to the Apostles and to the Christianity of the East."

Jack L. Arnold of Third Millenium Ministries sums

up succinctly on its website[1] the conventional wisdom
of Evangelical Protestantism about the Reformation-era
Church: "The Roman Catholic Church was theologically
sick and its theology led to atrocious corruptions. It was
spiritually exhausted, enfeebled, and almost lifeless. Rome
had seriously departed from the teaching of the Bible and
was engrossed in real heresy." On another site, www.just-
forcatholics.org, we find that the Catholic Church "at times
descended to the very pit of hell in corruption, greed, superstition, arrogance and crass immorality."

This view seems to be so entrenched in the modern
psyche as to be impervious to any alternative account. And
it is not just those with a vested interest in perpetuating the
33,000 or more sects that have been formed since the Reformation, all wearing the label "Christian," who continue
to parrot the collection of lies listed above. Even scholarly
works are often tainted, to the point that a reviewer of one
of the best recent Reformation studies (*The European Reformation*, by Professor Euan Cameron) felt obliged to point
out that "it is refreshing to find a text that does not start
from the premise that Protestantism was inevitable or even
desired by the laity."

As for the vast number of ministers and other personnel of the Protestant sects, they are naturally predisposed
to accept the version of history that they are taught in their
books and seminaries, and they pass it on to their flocks.
Years ago I asked a student where she had gotten a particularly egregious lie about the Church which she had
included in a paper, and she replied that she had learned

1 http://www.thirdmill.org/newfiles/jac_arnold/CH.Arnold.RMT.1.html

it in Sunday school. Patiently explaining the facts to her was a waste of my breath. Like countless Protestants, she just *knew* the Catholic Church had grown thoroughly rotten prior to Luther and company, and evidence to the contrary simply rolled off her.

I suppose many Protestants cling to this idea because it justifies their existence. If the Catholic Church had not been (and continues to be, of course) so corrupt and evil, what was the rationale for creating new churches? And secularists, naturally, are only too happy to buy into any version of history that paints the Church in a negative light. Absent a miracle of grace plus a degree of open-mindedness that is rarely to be found in such people, we cannot expect much objectivity these days about the pre-Reformation Catholic Church.

What of Catholics? Here the situation is almost as bad. Reformation myths are part of American culture, and it is a minority of Catholics today who remain unaffected by them. Poor formation is also to blame: twenty years ago, when I had just started teaching, some of my Catholic students told me they had learned more about their religion in my classes than they had ever been taught in either Catholic schools or religious education classes. I believe it; the state of catechesis and historical instruction in Catholic schools and other institutions declined precipitously in the 1960s and continues to present a very uneven picture. Today's Catholics are willing to believe any rot about the Church that they get from their textbooks, the media, or the air they breathe.

If, therefore, both Protestants and Catholics have bought into the lies about the Reformation, what are we to do? At the very least, we should first of all be sure we have our facts straight. Secondly, we need to realize just why it is that we make so little headway in countering the lies of history—and not just on this topic—and try to deal charitably with the obstacles we encounter.

The complex phenomenon known as the Reformation did not come out of nowhere. It was preceded by fifteen hundred years of Christian civilization, from the earliest Christian communities within the Roman Empire, through the slow conversion of barbarian Europe, to the high civilization of the Middle Ages. As discussed in a previous chapter, the medieval period saw the spectacular development of culture, education, social services, and humane political and economic institutions, and it included clouds of saints who were active in all areas of life.

The Difficult Centuries
Preceding the Reformation

The two centuries that immediately preceded the sixteenth, the century of the Reformation, were liberally punctuated with disasters of all kinds. The Hundred Years' War had sapped the energies of two major powers, England and France. It had particularly devastated France, formerly the center of European thought and culture. Climate change early in the fourteenth century brought debilitating famines, and these were followed by the greatest pandemic known to history until modern times: the Black Death, which brought with it social discord and a decline in morals. According to one contemporary chronicler, the plague was followed by a lowering in the quality (as well as the quantity, in many places) of clergy and religious. As the disease raged, the good and dedicated priests and religious ministered to the sick and buried the dead—thus contracting the plague themselves and dying. The not-so-dedicated, however, fled to isolated areas, where they managed to survive. They returned when the plague was over to fill the vacancies left by the heroic ones who had died.

The papacy also went through crisis after crisis during this black period. First it was the bitter quarrel between Pope Boniface VIII—not one of the shining examples of a pontiff—and the French crown over taxation of the clergy, which led to a confrontation between the Pope, a French delegation, and a group of the Pope's Italian political enemies. Which of them (probably it was the Italians) actually laid hands on the elderly Pontiff and pushed him around in the office of his vacation residence is unclear, but he returned to Rome much shaken and died shortly after the incident. The next Pope, a Frenchman, never left France and instead established the papal court at Avignon, where it remained for nearly seventy years. The move made sense from a number of angles, but there was no getting away from the fact that Peter had left Rome, and Christendom was scandalized. (Keep in mind that the war, the plague, and the nasty climate change were going on at the same time.)

At Avignon, Church government was often carried on very efficiently, but the anomalous situation precluded grand plans such as the calling of a council to deal with the extraordinary evils of the time. As Christopher Dawson points out in *The Dividing of Christendom,* the efficiency of the Avignon papacy's taxation system went hand in hand with a decline in its prestige and power within

Christendom, for it grew scandalously wealthy and increasingly secularized. Finally, largely due to the "nagging" (the Pope's word) of St. Catherine of Siena, Pope Gregory XI returned to Rome in 1377. Now Church life and activity could return to normal—except that the war was still raging, the Turks were still raiding the coasts, and dislocation was still affecting many areas of European life.

A return to normalcy would have been nice, but it did not happen. The Pope died soon after his return, and the next Pope elected was quickly rejected by a group of cardinals who had second thoughts when they saw what a harsh reformer he was going to be. They decided they did not want him after all and proceeded to elect another man. Thus began the Great Schism of the West, which was to go on into the following century, consistently producing two and sometimes three claimants to the papal throne, complete with their own courts and groups of cardinals. Few in Europe knew who the true pope was, and there were saints on opposite sides of the issue. Furthermore, as Dawson remarks, the scandal of the Avignon papacy had not been eliminated but rather doubled or even tripled depending on the number of "papal" courts there were in existence at any one time.

In the early fifteenth century, things seemed to be looking up. The Hundred Years' War ended, with Joan of Arc rallying France to drive out the English and with the final victories of the French after her death (the English went home to start the Wars of the Roses), and the Council of Basel finally ended the Western Schism. Some members of that council, however, began to argue that since they had solved the problem of three popes (by choosing one of them), the council itself was the ultimate authority in the Church: this was the heresy of Conciliarism. It took time for that error to be squashed. Basel also had to deal with the ongoing heretical movement in Bohemia that stemmed from the preaching of Jan Hus, who in turn had been considerably influenced by the heresy of the Englishman John Wycliffe.

It is little wonder that the popes, once back in Rome and picking up the pieces, found it safer to deal mostly with local issues, and in particular, their positions as Italian princes trying to restore and order the territories of the Holy See. Seduced by the glories of the High Renaissance and its worldly culture, they burned rigorous carpers like Savanarola and seem to have been less aware than their medieval predecessors, with their splendid diplomatic corps, of what was brewing in Germany, Bohemia, England, and even Italy.

What of conditions during the pre-Reformation years for ordinary Catholics in most of Europe? It is not entirely clear how the lives of ordinary Catholics were affected by the Western Schism, apart from the profound scandal it gave. Certainly the leadership and social services provided by local dioceses must have suffered from the fact that for many decades no one was sure who the true pope was. Parallel institutions were sometimes set up by rival claimants to the papal throne, but the lack of unity must have compromised the efficient operation of all those institutions of education and welfare that had been among the great achievements of the institutional Church. As in the dark period of the tenth century, Catholics in pre-Reformation Europe complained about the ignorance and immorality of many priests, about the too-great influence of political authorities in church affairs, about the worldliness of many of the upper clergy (who were only imitating some of the popes), and about the lack of thoroughgoing reform. Things for the most part had not been nearly as bad as in the tenth century, but now increased literacy and, by the mid-fourteenth century, the invention of the printing press allowed for discontent to spread more widely. There were, meanwhile, always individual heretics peddling their own brand of "reform," always local political leaders who attempted to control ecclesiastical finances, and always the tendency of monarchs to want to free themselves from the restraints on their actions that the Church often imposed (sometimes, it must be admitted, imprudently).

These were more or less perennial gripes, as were the complaints about the heavy tithes and other taxes that various Church institutions levied on the faithful. It is possible that conditions such as the Black Death and subsequent upheavals had in fact increased the need of the Church for money to meet increased demands for welfare services, but that was hardly the fault of either the Church or the ordinary people.

Despite all these problems, in the pre-Reformation period there were still saints, including St. Catherine of Siena, St. Bridget of Sweden, and the great preacher St. Vincent Ferrer. If ever there was a saint for the times, it was Vincent. For over twenty years he criss-crossed Europe, preaching and fighting for souls. He called himself "the Angel of the Judgment" and warned that the end of the world really was very near if people did not repent. Vast numbers did so at his preaching. During this period, Church institutions still cared for the poor and the sick and taught the young in schools, and the Sacraments were still administered by priests who, on the whole, did their jobs adequately even if they were not as learned as they should have been. Preachers from monastic orders still preached, and if ecclesiastical con men like Chaucer's Pardoner still tried to sell pardons and other spiritual favors to the gullible, that was not a new development in history.

Pre-Reformation Heresies

Nor was the persistence of heresy a new development. Those medieval Cathars, Patarenes, and other groups left over from the medieval centuries had not completely died out. There may not have been fanatics starving themselves to death because they had become so "perfect," but there were people throughout the fourteenth and fifteenth centuries who hung onto some of the ideas of those medieval heretics. The twelfth-century "poor men" in the area of France around Lyon who followed a certain Valdes, later known as Peter Waldo, were one such group. Valdes seems to have had a conversion to a more intense spiritual life, and he then made the decision to get rid of his considerable wealth and live a life of absolute poverty in accordance with the teachings of the Gospels. He was joined by other seekers after perfection, and they began to preach to others. Here they soon went off the rails due to their general lack of education; they often misunderstood scriptural passages and ended by denying teachings concerning the existence of Purgatory and prayers for the dead, among other things.

Seeking an elusive legitimacy, these "Waldensians" sought to give themselves a pedigree dating back to the early Church, though there was no evidence for such a lineage. They forbade the taking of oaths—which may indicate Cathar influence—and refused to obey when they were ordered to stop preaching. The Inquistor Bernard Gui's account of interrogating a member of this sect shows just how exasperating and subtle they could be: "Questioned as to whom he [the Waldensian] considers a good Christian, he replies, 'He who believes as Holy Church teaches him to believe.' When he is asked what he means by 'Holy Church,' he answers, 'My lord, that which you say and believe is the Holy Church.' If you say to him, 'I believe that the Holy Church is the Roman Church over which the lord pope rules, and under him, the prelates,' he replies, 'I believe it,' meaning that he believes that you believe it." If required to swear under oath to the truths of the Faith, Waldensians employed various stratagems, such as stammering over the oath or inserting words and omitting others, so that in the end they had not sworn at all. One Waldensian frankly admitted that he would swear in order to escape prosecution and then do penance for it later.

Excommunicated, the Waldensians continued their existence outside the Church and proved a handy support for the future efforts of the sixteenth-century Protestants, while spreading to most of the countries of Eastern and Western Europe. The Waldensian ideas on radical poverty, vernacular translations of the Bible, and lay preaching would appear in England during the late fourteenth century in the thought of John Wycliffe and his followers. When Wycliffe (or Wyclif), a teacher at Oxford University, began to deny Transubstantiation, he alienated some of his followers (called Lollards) as well as the Church authorities, but seems to have escaped excommunication. Lollardy, which later became connected with sometimes-violent political discontent, seems to have survived into the sixteenth century, but it was not a major factor in the continuation of Wycliffian heresy. That heresy would be, improbably, carried on at the other end of Europe, in Bohemia; a royal marriage was the vehicle by which it had traveled there.

Anne of Bohemia was the wife of the English King Richard II. Upon her death in 1394, her servants returned to their native land, bringing with them the new ideas of John Wycliffe that they had absorbed during their sojourn in England. It was apparently from them, or from Bohemian students who had studied in England, that a young Bohemian cleric named Jan Hus became familiar with—and much intrigued by—the ideas of Wycliffe. Ordained a priest in 1400 at the age of thirty-one and zealous for Church reform, Hus must have known that many of Wycliffe's propositions had been condemned. He nevertheless translated a number of his works into Czech and propagated them, though he submitted to a later correction of them by Church authorities. The situation was complicated by the Western Schism and the attempts to end it by means of a council, but in the end Hus was excommunicated for heresy.

Conditions in Bohemia were both politically and religiously complex, and the numerous followers of Jan Hus, like the Lollards of England, sometimes engaged in violence. Hus himself was popular in his country because of his patriotism, supporting Bohemian nationalism against German influence, and because of his zeal for Church reform and for the Faith, as he understood it. Finally, taking the advice of Sigismund, Holy Roman Emperor, Hus decided to put his case before the Council of Constance in 1415. At the council, Pope John XXIII[2] lifted his excommunication but forbade him to say Mass until his case was settled. Hus declared himself ready to retract any of his errors, but incredibly, he continued not only saying Mass but preaching as well—a deliberate provocation of the Pope. Despite the safe conduct issued by the Emperor, Hus was arrested, imprisoned, and tried. Both the Bohemians and the Poles present protested at the irregularities of the imprisonment and trial and the violation of the safe conduct, but it went forward. Hus denied writing some of the statements of which he was accused and defended others—including propositions that Wycliffe had also supported. He refused to retract those, was condemned, and then burned at the stake. Opinion is divided on the legitimacy of the trial and execution, with some arguing that the safe conduct was not intended to protect Hus against legal prosecution and punishment. In any case, the consequences of the Hus affair would be grave.

Here we can see the emergence of one of the many features of the Reformation that are not strictly religious. In this case it is nationalism, which would play a great role in the rise of most of the new Protestant religions. Hus immediately became a Bohemian hero; he was constantly invoked in the later Hussite Wars of the heretical (and patriotic) Bohemians against the Catholic emperors who were attempting to control both the country and the heresy.

In 1512 Pope Julius II called the Fifth General Council

---

2 This John XXIII (1410-1415) is today considered an antipope, a false claimant to the papacy.

of the Lateran, largely to deal with various political quarrels both outside and within the Church. He died in 1513, and his successor, Leo X (Medici), continued the council for his own goals. It met only a dozen times, and although it made a few good rulings and addressed the need for some reforms, it was by no means the spearhead of reform that it could have been. By an eerie coincidence, the sessions wound up in 1517, just a few months before Luther burst onto the religious scene. It would be nearly thirty years before another council—the great Council of Trent—would take up at last the Protestant challenge and galvanize the movement for true Catholic reform.

There was thus a general sense in the Church before the Protestant Reformation—as there has probably been at most times in Church history—that some things should be fixed because they were out of kilter. But of a broad consensus among pre-Reformation Catholics for a dismantling of the Church and the creation of a new one there was no trace.

Conditions in England before the Reformation

In an earlier chapter we have seen the development of guilds during the Middle Ages and the vital economic, social, and political role they played in the new towns that were part of the medieval revival of Europe after the Dark Ages. This topic has been explored in depth by Eamon Duffy in his *The Stripping of the Altars: Traditional Religion in England 1400-1580.* A review of the book by Christopher Harper-Bill in *Theology* lauds this "brilliant study" as "essential reading for all those who wish to understand late medieval religion and the means by which it was undermined against the wishes of the vast majority of its practitioners." That is the essential point: the Catholic religion of the masses was destroyed *against their wishes*. The Protestant Reformation was a *revolution*, and as another historian has remarked of revolutions, they are never really made by "the people." Certainly in England the changes brought by the religious revolution, far from being desired by the English people, were bitterly resented.

It was King Henry VIII who first broke with the Catholic Church in England—because it would not declare his valid marriage invalid and permit him to marry Anne Boleyn. Thus began the "Church of England" and Anglicanism. The need for money and support led Henry to take measures against the guilds and monasteries, as described below. Under his son Edward, a minor, Protestant advisors proliferated in the government, and still more anti-Catholic measures were introduced. Following the brief reign of Henry's Catholic daughter, Mary, who provided a respite from Protestant persecution but was unable to restore the country to its pre-Henry state, the formidable Queen Elizabeth I, flanked by her even more formidable minister, William Cecil, and her sinister "interrogator" and torturer Topcliffe, instituted full-scale persecution of the Church and confiscation of the assets of recalcitrant Catholic families. This escalation of royal violence against all things Catholic began with Henry's attacks on the guilds and the monasteries.

In addition to their economic functions, the English guilds (generally spelled "gilds" in England) also had important spiritual and religious functions, and all their various features were harmoniously incorporated into the lives of their members. By the later Middle Ages, such guilds still operated in the towns and cities of England, but there were also numerous "guilds" in the countryside that were primarily devotional in character. These confraternities kept up pious practices such as maintaining a light in the parish church before the image of the guild's patron saint and praying for the souls of deceased guildsmen. Members contributed sums for funerals and Masses for their deceased, and they also paid for the funerals of poor members. They might also help with the expenses of members who were ill or needed financial relief for some other reason (provided it was not their own fault!), and sometimes they supported the parish schools.

These religious customs and practices were so closely entwined with the daily lives of ordinary people that over the centuries they had become almost part of themselves. In particular, the ceremonies and prayers for the dead, the processions—which assumed a civic character for the town that hosted them, the Advent customs, and the ceremonies of Holy Week marked the seasons of the year and gave them a sacred character and importance that no mere calendar could do. All these things, and any others that smacked of Catholic piety, became targets of the Anglican liturgical police.

Protestant Devastation in England

Since devotion to Our Lady was very strong in England, the Rosary naturally had to be suppressed. There is the story of Elizabeth's liturgical police visiting a village church and finding an old woman there saying the Rosary. One of the "superstition"- hunters seized the beads and broke them, pushing around the protesting woman in the process. The villagers ganged up on the aggressor and beat him, possibly killing him as well. Such incidents occurred sporadically throughout England, but in every case the Catholic people failed to hold off the authorities for long.

The English Reformation was a disaster for the guilds in every way. Henry VIII confiscated their funds, and Elizabeth issued statutes that worked to cripple them. During the reign of Henry's son Edward VI, who came to the throne at the age of nine in 1547, the apostate Archbishop Cranmer and his Protestant associates proceeded to establish Protestantism more firmly in England than Henry had permitted, and one of their targets was the guilds. It is estimated that during the 1530s and 1540s, thousands of guilds were suppressed and their resources, including land if they had any, confiscated. The demoralizing effect of the loss of their beloved confraternities and professional organizations was devastating for the guildsmen of the time. In the long term, the disappearance of such associations meant that by the beginning of the Industrial Revolution in the eighteenth century, brutalized workers had no organization to speak for them or to buffer the misery of their squalid lives.

The guilds were not the only target chosen to provide the funds Henry needed—in part to bribe supporters to rally to his new church. The monasteries were to be "visited" to make sure they were not corrupt, and they were to be suppressed if they were—all in the interest of maintaining the purity of religious life, of course. Cardinal Wolsey had already "dissolved" some twenty-nine religious establishments in the 1520s, and in 1535 it was Thomas Cromwell, Henry's vicar, who escalated and completed the despoiling and destruction of English monastic life.

Were the monasteries corrupt? Certainly there was some

moral corruption in some monasteries, as there has been at most times in history, but that could have been easily dealt with on a case-by-case basis. Other visitations during the same period, by local authorities, had turned up nothing very damning. Rooting out real corruption was not, however, the goal of Henry and his servants; if it had been, they might have expected to find it in the larger and wealthier religious houses rather than in the smaller and poorer ones. The former, however, had more political influence, and Cromwell was loath to attack them at first. The "visitors" sent out by Henry and Cromwell in 1535, then, went first to the nearly four hundred smaller religious houses known as the "lesser monasteries." These visitors made a show of seeking out moral corruption (extracting surprisingly few admissions of it, and those mostly obtained under pressure) and trying to persuade young religious to abandon their vocations. At the same time, preachers were sent out in a propaganda campaign to attack and disparage monastic life.

In February 1536, Parliament simply dissolved the lesser monasteries. A few were allowed to survive and, surprisingly, the inmates—the same monks and nuns whose reputations had already been blackened—were now declared to be exemplary religious. (The act of Parliament also specified that the inhabitants of the greater monasteries were beyond reproach. Moral corruption as an issue seems to have disappeared.) The lesser houses were looted, and their funds and lands went to the Crown; Henry was pleased but not yet satisfied. There remained the larger, wealthier monasteries. The rising of the north of England in the Pilgrimage of Grace in October 1536, motivated partially by a desire to save the remaining monasteries as well as to preserve the Faith in England, delayed Henry's plans, though not for long. Soon the goods and lands of *all* the monasteries were in his hands; the land in particular he used as bribes to his courtiers, merchants, lawyers, and others.

Leaving aside the spiritual loss to England—in preaching, teaching, and prayer (not to mention the heresy, the suppression of the Holy Sacrifice, the loss of souls)—what of the schools, hospitals, orphanages, guesthouses, homes for widows, and other services the monasteries had provided? Protestant writer William Cobbett, writing in the nineteenth century, declared that the dissolution of the monasteries had the effect of making not merely poverty but "pauperism" a permanent condition of the English lower classes. University education suffered too, since poor students no longer had the support the monks had provided; the gap between upper and lower classes widened. Peasants were driven to misery by the loss of the monastery lands they had been allowed to use for farming and grazing.

In the cities, the secular clergy had also engaged in teaching and other services for the poor, services paid for by the tithes they collected—those tithes that were so much attacked by would-be "reformers." As Euan Cameron, a Protestant scholar and professor, put it in his excellent 1991 work, *The European Reformation,* "Had the London secular clergy given up their tithes and lived off alms (as some Carmelite friars urged in the 1460s) many valuable activities, including education and poor relief must have suffered."

The final result was that Protestantism triumphed in England, and its propaganda became accepted in place of the age-old Catholic Faith and customs. To quote Duffy once more, "By the end of the 1570s, whatever the instincts and nostalgia of their seniors, a generation was growing up which had known nothing else, which believed the pope to be Antichrist, the Mass a mummery, which did not look back on the Catholic past as their own, but another country, another world."

Protestant Devastation on the Continent

Elsewhere in Europe, newly Protestantized areas suffered similar disruption. The quality of public institutions regressed from their medieval levels. James J. Walsh observes that modern writers have tended to assume, on the basis of the deplorable hospitals and asylums of their own time (the early 1900s and the 1800s), that medieval ones must have been much worse; the assumption was that the further back one goes, the more ignorant and barbaric the conditions were bound to have been. Walsh's research revealed, however, that the opposite was often the case. Looking at medical progress in the late Middle Ages, he found great advances in medical education, clinical study, pharmacology, and health regulations based on the new knowledge of the time. He records advances and experiments in all types of surgery: bone, cosmetic, obstetrical, heart, and intestinal, as well as the treatment of gunshot wounds (a new problem, caused by the invention of gunpowder). There is even mention of the use of anesthesia, about which there was some controversy, with some surgeons using it and others disapproving. (The practice was eventually given up and the technique lost until modern times.)

As for the hospitals, Walsh states that the worst hospitals in history—vastly inferior to their medieval counterparts—were those built in the early nineteenth century. Those buildings, squalid, dark, and overcrowded, were truly dismal places for a sick person to have to go to. The medieval hospitals, on the other hand, whether for the poor or for wealthy patients, were attractive, spacious buildings with large windows, often set in gardens and near a source of water for sanitation. Patients were nursed by dedicated religious trained in medicine; the wealthy paid for their medicine and for their food and wine, which they had brought in to them, but the poor paid nothing for those things. The walls of the cubicles or rooms were covered with paintings or other decorations so that the patients had something attractive to look at. Institutions for the mentally ill were similarly advanced; they were by no means the "snake pits" of early modern horror stories. In northern Europe the insane were generally housed in hospitals attached to monasteries in rural areas, with each patient given plenty of room and gently treated. Spain was considered to be particularly advanced in the treatment of the insane, and patients often improved to the point that they could be returned to society.

The Reformation had a devastating effect on hospitals and all other forms of social service, as we have seen above in the cases of the monasteries and the guilds. One author of a history of nursing wrote that only in religious orders did knowledge of nursing and nursing skills survive. Eventually the Protestant state would have to provide for the indigent, the ill, the orphaned, and the insane within its borders, but that took time, and the resulting public institutions left much to be desired when compared with what the Church had for centuries provided out of love of God.

As for education, Erasmus, who was originally sympathetic to some of the aims of the "Reformers," wrote, "Where Lutheranism reigns, there is an end of letters." He was referring to the closing of schools and universities when their persecuted personnel were forced to flee. The disappearance of all these institutions, when the religious orders staffing them were suppressed, caused great hardship. They too would eventually be restored as state institutions. However a German or English student suddenly prevented from taking his degree, or a sick person evicted from a Church hospital, would certainly have told you that conditions were a great deal better before the Reformation than after it.

Then there were the monastic treasures of art and architecture, of which the value is incalculable. A hospital would eventually be replaced, though it might not be of the same quality as its predecessor, but the priceless stained-glass windows and precious reliquaries (to say nothing of their even more precious contents) smashed by Protestant mobs could never be reproduced. The tombs of Catholic kings perished also. When the monasteries were suppressed in England, mobs were on hand to loot them, and there are reports of these louts using the manuscripts from the wrecked libraries to wipe their boots—manuscripts that might have taken a monk a lifetime to copy and illuminate with pictures. Artistically, then, the Protestant areas of Europe were likewise much worse off after the Reformation than before.

Other Consequences of the Reformation

It is politics that was often the key to the emergence and survival of the new religions. In England, Henry VIII, and to a greater extent Elizabeth I, linked their political power, wealth, and international influence to their control of religion. This was true on the continent of Europe also, since many of the German princes joined the Reformation movement for what they, and the territory they represented, could get out of it politically. The new Protestant religion of the Dutch would be one motive for their rebellion against their Spanish Catholic overlords. "In the sixteenth century," writes Cameron, "religion became mass politics."

The longer-term cultural and psychological consequences of the Reformation in Europe and England are not our topic here, but it is worth keeping in mind that those consequences were so devastating that even some modern Protestants have come to regret what their forerunners accomplished. Walsh, in his *The Thirteenth, Greatest of Centuries,* quotes a German dramatist discussing the cultural rupture caused by the Reformation: "I, as a Protestant, have often had to regret that we purchased our freedom of conscience, our individual liberty, at entirely too high a price. In order to make room for a small, mean little plant of personal life, we destroyed a whole garden of fancy and hewed down a virgin forest of aesthetic ideas. We went even so far in the insanity of our weakness as to throw out of the garden of our souls the fruitful soil that had been accumulating for thousands of years, or else we plowed it under sterile clay."

The reference to "personal life" here introduces yet

another feature of the Reformation and the reason why it succeeded, and that is the essential *subjectivism* of Protestantism, exemplified in its principle of private judgment. Cameron points out that the Reformers succeeded in "subjecting doctrine to public debate; people were, in effect, invited to *choose* the religious ideas that appealed to them." Hence our modern subjectivism: I adhere to my religion not because I see that it is the only one founded by Christ, but because it happens to suit me.

There was a price for this radical shift in spiritual perspective. Protestant minister David Hartman in *The New Oxford Review* of September 28, 1989, wrote, "even for a Protestant preacher like me, it is hard to make an objective case that the overall state of human affairs has been improved by the Reformation. 'One of the great tragedies of human history,' the historian Paul Johnson has noted, 'and the central tragedy of Christianity—is the breakup of the harmonious world-order which had evolved, in the Dark Ages, on a Christian basis.'"

Fortunately, on the other side of the Protestant upheaval would come the real reformation, inaccurately known as the "Counter-Reformation". Pierre Janelle remarks that the Counter-Reformation "could hardly have succeeded, however, had Christendom been really corrupt at heart; but it was not . . . Christian Europe was rich in faith, charity, and devotion"—and it would give birth to another great age of the Church.

CHAPTER 7

A BLACK AND EXPEDIENT LEGEND

The Lie: The Spanish explorers of the New World were cruel and greedy, carrying out the orders of their Catholic masters and bringing untold misery to the peaceful Native Americans.

Here we come to a myth that exemplifies how historical lies often result from a combination of motives. The "Black Legend" says that the Spanish were historically a cruel and brutal people, as evidenced by the way they treated the native American tribes they conquered in the sixteenth century. The fact that the Conquistadors were Catholic made it worse: they and their missionaries viciously suppressed the religion and culture of highly civilized peoples such as the Aztecs, bringing death, disease, and servitude, while ramming Christianity down their throats.

This historical fairy tale was originally the product of English and Dutch political propaganda, and as such was motivated by nationalism and colonial rivalry in the New World as well as the religious fanaticism of the Protestant Reformation. Until quite recently, most English and American history textbooks, from elementary school through college, included some version of the Black Legend. For example, in the 1966 edition of *The American Nation: A History of the United States,* by Columbia University professor John A. Garraty, we learn that the Spanish conquerors "wrenched their empire from innocent hands; in an important sense, the settlement of America ranks among the worst examples of naked aggression in human history." A few years before, in 1959, a popular student history atlas informed young readers that the English colonial economy of the era depended on fishing and agriculture, whereas the Spanish preferred "mining, cattle raising, slavocracy"— and the statement was illustrated by a picture of a Spaniard holding a whip and directing slaves. Apparently there were no farmers in the Spanish colonies and no slaves in the English ones. That same year, readers of the *Saturday Evening Post,* curled up after dinner for a nice read, learned that the colonial Spanish had deliberately infected the Indians with smallpox to exterminate them.[1]

That the historiographical situation has begun to change a little in recent years is due to the work of a number of

---

1 This is a really egregious lie because the very opposite is true: as soon as smallpox vaccination was developed, the Spanish made it available to the Indians precisely because they were so vulnerable to the disease. It was the British in North America who infected blankets that they sent as gifts to their Indian enemies to kill them off. No vaccine for them!

well-trained historians who have challenged the Legend and sparked a welcome revision of this tired old tale. Such new scholarship on the origins, growth, and dissemination of the Legend shows how Anglo-Saxon attitudes have not only skewed our view of history but have also blighted our relations with South American countries. The focus of this chapter is on how the Legend describes Spain's conquests in the New World; I will discuss primarily the case of Spanish involvement in Mexico, since to Americans Mexico is more familiar than other colonies in South America.

The Historical Setting of the Black Legend

Following the final expulsion of the Moors from Spain by Ferdinand and Isabella in 1492, as well as their unification of the country and creation of a strong central monarchy, Spain entered into its golden age. The consequences of the discoveries of an obscure Genoese sailor, whose sailing expedition Isabella financed in that same fateful year, were to open an unsuspected new continent to Spanish colonization and provide an unheard-of bounty in precious metals and other resources. Spain would advance to new heights of wealth, power, and prestige in Europe.

Further to the north, the formerly dominant sea power, England, sulked at the emergence of its new rival and its success in the New World, and made efforts to stake its own claim to American lands. Unfortunately for the British seamen, there are no gold mines in Nova Scotia; the best the English achieved in their early expeditions was the discovery of good fishing spots. As the sixteenth century unfolded, so did more sources of friction between the northern and southern sea powers. By the end of the century Spain and

England were commercial, colonial, political, and religious rivals; for the second half of that century their rulers, Philip II and Elizabeth I, had been bitter personal rivals as well.

Philip had been married to Elizabeth's half-sister Mary Tudor during Mary's brief reign of five years as the only legitimate and only Catholic ruler of England to follow Henry VIII. Elizabeth, raised a Protestant, had promised Philip and Mary that when she succeeded to the throne she would allow Catholicism to continue to flourish in England. She broke that promise, however, as soon as Mary was dead and she herself was queen, speedily instituting her lengthy and appallingly cruel persecution of non-Anglicans. In the eyes of Philip, and of most of Europe, Elizabeth was not even the true sovereign of England because she was the illegitimate daughter of Henry and Anne Boleyn— and because Mary Stuart, the Catholic Queen of Scotland, had a far better claim to the throne (which is why Elizabeth would have her beheaded when she got the chance). Philip determined to support Mary.

Besides this political quarrel, there was Elizabeth's hated policy of sending out pirates to prey on Spanish colonies in the New World and on Spanish shipping. These buccaneers, the famous (or infamous) "Sea Dogs," were knighted for their exploits, which involved pillaging, killing, and enslaving peaceful Spanish settlers in the Caribbean, Florida, and elsewhere, as well as seizing Spanish treasure ships.

The religious rivalry between Elizabeth and Philip was a bitter one, and it affected their respective political positions in Europe. Philip became the Catholic champion of Europe in the face of Protestantism's spread, while Elizabeth supported the Protestant cause everywhere, for both political and religious reasons. Philip was also one of the Catholic champions of the West against the very grave assaults on Europe, by both land and sea, of the Ottoman Turks. England, on the other hand, had commercial alliances with the Turks, as did a series of Catholic French kings. This meant that when the most serious confrontations occurred between the West and the Turks, the two most powerful states of northwestern Europe remained neutral—unless we count the token force that France sent to the relief of Vienna in 1683, rather late in the day at that.

The Legend Takes Shape

The printing press would be a key factor in the growth and dissemination of the Black Legend. It meant that the English and the Dutch—a maritime people who also resented Spanish commercial success—could now churn out anti-Spanish propaganda in quantity. Some of the Dutch, converts to Protestantism, were also in revolt against Spain in the Spanish Netherlands, and thus they had a powerful political as well as economic reason to blacken the name of Spain. From presses in Holland and England, propaganda pamphlets spread all over Europe. Among the premises of the pamphleteers were that Spaniards were cruel, lazy, bigoted, and fanatical: so different from nice, well bred, benevolent Englishmen and Dutchmen, for example. The pamphlets were full of supposed Spanish atrocities in the New World and might include pictures of Spanish soldiers around a campfire roasting an Indian for dinner. (In one such picture, the buildings in the background—which are obviously Dutch in style—clearly betray the "report" as the work of someone who had never actually been there.) As the historian Philip Wayne Powell put it in his book *Tree of Hate: Propaganda and Prejudices Affecting United States Relations with the Hispanic World,* "The killing of Indians by Spaniards became 'atrocities,' or 'ruthless extermination'; but when Englishmen ran Irishmen to death by the thousands in their own bogs, or slaughtered them after surrender, this was called 'the Irish problem.'"

Indeed, although in contrast to alleged Spanish brutality we think fondly of the "Pilgrim fathers" having a cozy meal with Indians at Thanksgiving, relations between the English and the native Americans were not always friendly, either. The Puritan preacher Cotton Mather, who considered the Catholic Church "the kingdom of Antichrist," had similar thoughts about the Indians. When they began to die of disease in large numbers, probably due to their lack of immunity to germs the Europeans had brought with them to both North and South America, Mather rejoiced. The death of so many Indians, he said, would "make room for a better growth"— meaning more people like him. Under Governor Bradford, the Massachusetts settlers took revenge for the murder of a white trader by an Indian by massacring all the natives they could catch and then burning their bodies. Bradford described the "stink and stench" of the burning process, adding, "But the victory seemed a sweet sacrifice and they [the English] gave praise thereof to God." Oliver Cromwell, another Puritan, spoke in similar language of his slaughter of three thousand Irish in Ireland. The Puritan deity, it seems, was generally happy with the destruction of non-Puritans, especially if their bodies were burned.

It is often stated disparagingly that the Spanish went to the New World to find gold, as if that were proof of their cupidity and bad character. Finding gold, however, was also the mission the English government gave the first colonists at Jamestown, though in that project they were unlucky. What is also often overlooked is that the thinking of the time measured a nation's prosperity and status by its reserves of precious metals. (This would become a principle of the mercantilist system of a slightly later period.) One of the many goals of colonialism thus became the acquisition of gold and silver. Obviously individual colonists would have loved to fill their own pockets with the stuff, but insofar as both the Conquistadors and many of the English colonists were financed by their governments, looking for gold was part of their jobs; the Spanish were fortunate enough to succeed at it.

What Really Happened

When Cortez landed in Mexico in 1519 with about three hundred men, he had no clear idea of what awaited him except the belief that there was a fabulous and wealthy city somewhere inland, ruled by an emperor. As he made his way in the general direction of the city, he collected more information from the various Indian tribes he encountered, but nothing prepared him or his men for the reality of what he found.

Though one still comes across them, two popular myths have been fraying around the edges for some time. These are the early modern myth of the primitive "noble savage" in his paradise—a paradise which was unspoiled until the white man descended on it, and the myth of the highly civilized relatives of that savage, who were far ahead of Europeans in everything that mattered. The picture we have today of the conquest of Mexico by Cortes is a much more balanced view than the one that was common until the mid-twentieth century.

The civilization of the Aztecs, partially built on the earlier achievements of the Toltecs, was a curious mixture of elements. Aztec architecture and engineering had produced a capital city of such beauty and refinement, with its canals, gardens, and temples, that the Spaniards were in awe. Cortes' secretary, Bernal Diaz, recorded the opinion of some of the Spanish soldiers who had seen the great cities of Europe that, for variety of goods and efficient organization, there was nothing in those cities that could equal the great marketplace of Tenochtitlan (on the site of modern Mexico City).

The Aztecs were civilized, in short. Their civilization, however, like all civilizations, was based on their religion, and that was one of the most sinister cults to be found in all of history. Some recent historians suggest that some of the worst tenets of this religion had been created and were manipulated by a cynical and power-hungry Aztec official to ensure Aztec dominance over the other tribes in the region. In any case, the Aztecs practiced mass human sacrifice on the order of tens of thousands of victims a year in order to placate their gods. Many of the victims were captured during wars that the Aztecs provoked for that very purpose, while others were slaves. There were also many young children of Aztec families, who were chosen to be sacrificed to the god in charge of agricultural fertility. They were kept in nurseries for a short time before their deaths, then taken to the place of execution, where their throats were slit. Their tears were said to be a good sign of rain to come.

Most victims did not have it so easy. They were forced to climb the tall stepped pyramid to where a priest was waiting to cut their hearts from their chests and drop them, still beating, into the mouth of an idol. It was common for Aztec warriors to don the skins stripped off the bodies, still dripping with blood, and run through the streets. What remained of the sacrificial victims was thrown down the steps to be fed to animals or used for the cannibal feasts of both upper and lower classes. (Diaz, describing a dinner that Emperor Montezuma gave the Spaniards, remarks that Cortes passed up the meat course; he may have heard rumors of cannibalism from the non-Aztecs he met, or his suspicions about what was going on at the top of the pyramid may have been aroused quite soon after the Spanish arrived at Tenochtitlan, Montezuma's capital.)

These practices explain why, when some three hundred Spaniards landed in eastern Mexico, they were soon eagerly joined by tens of thousands of Indian tribesmen who had for too long been the prey of the victim-seeking Aztec warriors. Who actually made "the Conquest," if not these willing allies, who greatly outnumbered the Spanish themselves? In the early stages of relations with the Aztecs, the Spanish goal was not to conquer them but to establish friendly relations between them and the King of Spain. They naturally hoped also to convert the Aztecs from their diabolical religion to Christianity, but again, peacefully. When Cortes realized the truth about the human sacrifices, he took Montezuma prisoner and commanded him to order the cessation of the practice. This was done, but it also alienated the Aztec population, particularly the priestly caste. When Cortes had to leave Tenochtitlan temporarily, a fight broke out between Spanish and Aztecs during which Montezuma was killed by a stone apparently thrown by an Aztec—perhaps in retaliation for his stopping of the sacrifices.

For the Aztecs, the purpose of war was to take captives for human sacrifice; thus, when war broke out with the Spaniards, they themselves refused to surrender. The enemy would surely do to them what they did to their own prisoners. This tragic misapprehension, along with other profound differences in military tactics between the two sides, led to the unnecessary deaths of numerous Aztec warriors. Spanish casualties, on the other hand, did include captured Spanish soldiers who were sacrificed in a temple, their severed heads brought back to the battlefield and shown to their comrades. Cortes himself survived several instances in the final battle when he could easily have been slain; however, the Aztecs believed that an enemy leader must not be killed in battle but be taken captive and sacrificed. The warriors who managed to get close to Cortes seem to have quarreled over who was to get the credit for taking him—which allowed him to escape.

Historians still debate the question of how a small number of Spaniards in a totally unfamiliar land could have defeated the great Aztec Empire so easily and so thoroughly. Certainly, the large numbers of natives who joined the Spaniards out of hatred for Aztec cruelty were a major factor. In addition, the Spaniards possessed vast superiority in weaponry and tactics, particularly in siege warfare. Following the Spanish victory, Cortes rebuilt the largely destroyed capital and made grants of land to his own men, but also to prominent Aztecs. Self-governing native towns were set up in which Spaniards were neither to live nor to work. The Indians governed themselves using their native language (Nahuatl) and were required only to pay taxes and allow missionaries to visit them. Except for a small number of prisoners of war, Cortes allowed no slavery, and King Philip III later abolished all Indian personal servitude and employment on sugar plantations. By 1539 the Pope had excommunicated anyone guilty of enslaving or robbing the Indians. We might pause here to consider whether any previous conquest in history has ever proceeded thus, or whether the later English and Americans behaved similarly in their conquests of the North American Indians. (To raise the question is to answer it.)

But surely there has to be some fire behind the propaganda smoke of Spanish abuses? There was, of course, though nothing on the scale alleged by the enemies of Spain. Some of the successors of Cortes as governor were unusually cruel and greedy, and the King of Spain was far away. Much of the difficulty in dealing with abuses in the colonies—as with all colonies of any nation—stemmed from the length of time needed for communication with governmental authorities in the mother country. To deal with this problem, the King appointed the Bishop of Mexico as "Protector of the Indians." The first holder of that title smuggled evidence of wrongdoing against the local Spanish governor back to Spain in a sailor's pack; the governor was replaced.

Abuses there were, but benefits abounded also. Under Cortes, the first hospital for Indians was established, and by 1534 there were schools for Indian girls. In 1539 the first printing press in the New World was set up, printing translations of all sorts of writings for the Indians. Orphanages, trade schools, and colleges followed, and even a university for Aztec students, founded in 1551. The curriculum was modeled on that of Salamanca, and the Aztecs proved to be diligent students. When the first class graduated, the Spanish tried to turn the school over to them, to run it themselves for their own people. This seems to have been less than successful; the Aztecs might be brilliant students, but at that point they still lacked certain management and organizational skills. Those skills would come, however, to the point that a full-blooded descendent of Montezuma was later appointed viceroy of Mexico by the Spanish king. Racist the Spanish were not.

Treatment of Indians after the Conquest

From the first discoveries in the New World, scholarly debate had raged in Spain as to the nature of the inhabitants of the various parts of the vast new lands. The sophisticated Aztecs with their advanced civilization were clearly human, however much their religion might be demonic. In the case of some Stone Age tribes in Central America that were fleetingly encountered by the Conquistadors, the case was unclear; those people were so unlike any human race known to the Spanish. These questions were hashed out in great philosophical, theological, and practical detail, because provisions had to be made for the treatment and just governance of these new Spanish subjects. The conclusions were clear and uncompromising, marking a new advance for the Western world: the Indians were human beings created by God, they possessed human rights, and they must be treated justly.

These Catholic thinkers took seriously the statement of Pope Paul II in 1537 that the Indians should not "be treated like irrational animals and used exclusively for our profit and our service . . . [They] must not be deprived of their freedom and their possessions . . . even if they are not Christians; and on the contrary, they must be left to enjoy their freedom and their possessions." The Pope emphasized the Christian principle that "Every person is my brother or sister." (I will not spin out the obvious comparison between this Catholic view of the rights of indigenous peoples, which the French colonists in North America also shared, and the manner in which the English and their descendents viewed the Indians they had to deal with. Who was it who said, "The only good Indian is a dead Indian"?)

In the first years following the conquest, conversions of the Aztecs and other Mexican tribes to Christianity proceeded only slowly, despite the best efforts of dedicated Franciscan missionaries. Particularly in areas where there was little governmental presence, relations between Spanish colonists and the Indians were often strained, and this evidently hindered the natives' receptivity to the religion of the white man. In 1531, however, came the mysterious and instantaneous appearance of the image of a young woman—clearly the Virgin Mary—on the cloak of a middle-aged Aztec.

This man, Juan Diego, was bringing to the Bishop a bouquet of roses, flowers miraculously given to him by a young woman who had appeared to him a number of times and asked that the Bishop build a church to her. When Juan Diego, after much hassle, came into the presence of the Bishop and allowed his rolled-up *tilma*—cloak—to fall open, he was startled to see all those present kneel down in veneration: on the *tilma* was an extraordinary image of Our

Lady of Guadalupe. Scientific analysis has not revealed any way by which the image could have been produced. It was not painted (although it has been touched up with paint over the centuries); the cloth should have disintegrated within a generation but is still in perfect condition over four centuries after it first appeared; high magnification shows figures in the eye of the image, as if they were reflected in a living eye at the moment the image was captured; and these are only some of the features of this legendary relic. Most singularly, the image resembles a pregnant Aztec woman and includes symbols that conveyed a spiritual message to the Aztecs. From the time the image first appeared, miracles were associated with it, and within six years some eight million Aztecs had been converted to the Catholic Faith.

The importance of this mass conversion cannot be overemphasized. Conquered and conquerors now shared a common religion. Since the Spanish were not, like the English, racially prejudiced, they were now willing to intermarry with the natives, eventually producing a far more racially homogenous society than ever existed north of Mexico. This sort of thing was simply not done, at least in any great numbers, by the discriminating English. (Here someone will say "Pocahontas!" That's one.)

The Black Legend Lives On

I have given a sketch of Spanish behavior in the Americas in some detail because it became the main feature of the Black Legend, whether in sixteenth-century Holland and England or in American textbooks until very recently. Were the Spaniards unusually greedy and cruel—compared with their English colonial rivals, for example? Did the

Church violate natives' rights in its zeal for souls? I think the record speaks for itself. Atrocities there have been in all colonial enterprises, and on the side of both the colonists and the colonized, but these were hardly limited to one nation. (There were dreadful reports about German colonists in Venezuela, but no one seems to mention those.) The Church's solicitude for the Indians, in both the spiritual and the material sense, was praiseworthy.

Of course, Spanish success in the New World is not the only component of the Legend; there are others. For example, Spain often had authoritarian rulers. Franco ruled Spain not so long ago, and in the liberal view, that just goes to show you. Historically, the country has been zealously Catholic, which is also a black mark in modern, secular historiography.

One of the first revisionist works on the Black Legend to be published in the United States is *Tree of Hate: Propaganda and Prejudices Affecting United States Relations with the Hispanic World,* by Philip Wayne Powell, mentioned earlier. This wide-ranging treatment of the topic discusses modern prejudices as well as criticisms of the original conquest. Ironically, as Powell points out, the nineteenth-century liberation movement in Spanish America, which threw off the rule of Spain and produced the numerous independent states of modern South and Central America, also adopted a version of the Black Legend to suit its own political purposes. This version pitted supposed Spanish political oppression and the domination of racially Spanish colonists against native or mixed-race peoples. Whether things are now wonderful in the liberated states may be questioned. President Teddy Roosevelt, who took a dim view of non-Anglo-Saxons anyway, considered that because the United States was a "civilized nation," it must fight "chronic wrongdoing" throughout the Western hemisphere. The Spanish-American War and Roosevelt's "taking" of Panama, along with Taft's "dollar diplomacy," were all supposed to make Hispanics more like North Americans. Wilson's "missionary diplomacy," particularly in Cuba and Haiti, was intended to show those backward Hispanics "how to elect good men." It is little wonder that American Hispanophobia, for so long a staple of our schools and textbooks, often provokes a corresponding antipathy and distrust in the Hispanic world.

As far as the original Spanish colonization goes, however, we can concur with Lewis Hanke that no European nation, possibly excepting Portugal, "took her Christian duty toward native peoples so seriously as did Spain." It is a great achievement.

CHAPTER 8

AND THERE ARE MORE . . .

The lies discussed in the chapters of this book are only some examples, though perhaps the most familiar ones, of the distortion of history by anti-religious bias. Many more illustrations could be given, among them the ongoing attacks on the Catholic Church—and on Pope Pius XII in particular—for supposedly not doing enough to prevent the Holocaust or to save Jews from it. The argument is that the Pope not only did not do nearly enough to help the Jews persecuted by the Nazi regime during World War II, but that he actually sympathized with Nazi goals. The proof—and almost the only fact adduced—is that so many Jews died.

The illogic of this charge is startling. No only does it assume what would have to be proven, but it attributes to the Church an extraordinary degree of power that it has never possessed or claimed. Only an omnipotent supranational organism, with the physical power to back up its decrees, could by mere force of will stop any large-scale atrocity whatsoever. Certainly the League of Nations was unable to do any such thing, and the record of the United Nations is little better. The interesting thing about this particular lie is that it was only developed decades after World War II, in direct contradiction to the praise given to the Pope and the Church by Jews immediately after the war. Pinchas Lapide, historian and Israeli consul to the Holy See, estimated that some 860,000 Jews were saved by the Catholic Church during the war, far more than the number saved by all other nations and groups put together. On another front, the Pope was personally in favor of the overthrow of Hitler, and he both encouraged the secret German resistance and saw that Vatican agents passed on information to Allied agents. The idea that he was in any way pro-Hitler is ridiculous.

A related charge is that the Vatican was responsible for hiding Nazi criminals after the war and helping them escape. The total absence of evidence for this does not seem to matter to the purveyors of the lie; they know that one cannot prove a negative proposition, so denials of the vicious charge do not stop it from circulating.

Yet another lie, this one mostly concerning earlier centuries, is that the Catholic Church supported slavery. In fact, the Church was involved for centuries in the struggle to free slaves, and the first author of an abolitionist work was a Jesuit priest in Cartagena, a major port for the South American slave trade in the seventeenth century. As early as 1435, when the Portuguese who had reached the Canary Islands were enslaving the inhabitants, the Pope condemned the practice and the slaves were ordered freed. The very transformation of Europe from the slavery-based Roman Empire to the nations of Christendom espousing rights for all classes is evidence of the liberating character of Catholicism.

A very broad-reaching lie that covers all of history, from the emergence of Christianity until the present, involves the position of women. In a word: women were always downtrodden, treated as less than human, and refused their rightful place in all things, including the Church. I have not tackled this lie in the present volume because it would require a volume of its own. I deal with it in my college courses, and in Appendix 2 I have included a couple of books dealing with women in the Middle Ages. Simply put, the idea that women were oppressed in the early Church is idiocy. St. Paul had proclaimed a spiritual equality between men and women ("no longer male nor female, slave nor free"), and he had women helpers. Women are major figures in the Gospels, and we know they held positions in the early Church; that they were not priests is irrelevant.

Under persecution, women often showed amazing courage. In Lyon the slave girl Blandina, whom her Christian companions had expected to crack under torture, proved so steadfast that even the pagans were saying they had never seen a woman suffer so much and so bravely. In Carthage it was another slave girl, Felicitas, and her friend Perpetua, an aristocrat, who faced martyrdom so courageously as to move the spectators in the arena where they met their deaths. (We have Perpetua's diary, which records the story of her imprisonment until her final day. Christian women were writers too.) Emperor Constantine's mother Helena was certainly a prominent Christian woman; and during the ages that followed Rome's fall, there are too many great Catholic ladies, both religious and laywomen, even to list here. Where feminists get the idea that women were oppressed or invisible during this time is beyond me.

In the Middle Ages, women were teachers, nurses, artists, authors, mystics, and even doctors. They were businesswomen with guilds of their own. They were saintly nuns and saintly wives and queens, as well as non-saintly but certainly powerful political figures like Eleanor of Aquitaine. Finally, Joan of Arc—of whom there is no male equivalent.

We will never be able to extinguish the seven lies discussed in this book, and all the rest of them; no matter what we do, the lies will continue to circulate in one form or another—and others will join them. In the first place, they are simply too useful to the Church's enemies. It should also be evident, from a survey of the varied topics we have covered, that most purveyors of these lies are extraordinarily close-minded. Leaving aside the few men of good will who have simply gotten the facts wrong and are willing to look at historical truth if it is shown to them, the liars do not want to be convinced. They are impatient with our demonstrations because the truth or falsity of their accusations is really not the point. The point is to discredit the Catholic Church. The one urging them on, whether they know it or not, is the Father of Lies, who is endlessly inventive when it comes to providing ammunition to his dupes. The purveyors of lies then proceed to write college textbooks, to give lectures, to post news articles on the Internet, and to author tomes that people like themselves promote onto the bestseller list.

But what is it, exactly, that produces such hostility to the Catholic Church, particularly in our own age? There is obviously something about us Catholics that modern intellectuals cannot stomach, and what that is seems to be the premise that the authority of the Church comes from a supernatural source: God Himself. Rejecting the source, they try by all possible means to discredit the institution that claims to speak for the source. Parenthetically, let us distinguish the doctrine that the Church today teaches what she has always taught in matters of faith and morals, from the idea that nothing can ever change in the Church. No one argues that nothing can ever change in the Church. Matters of discipline such as the Imprimatur and the Index and the Inquisition can be changed without compromising doctrine, and these changes are no indication that the Church was "wrong" when the discipline was otherwise. (Neither, of course, is anyone obliged to stand up and cheer for every disciplinary change. One is also quite free, for example, to think that a tougher attitude toward heretics within the Church today would be a very good thing.)

The Catholic claim to possess absolute truth from God (in certain limited areas) is totally alien to the modern mind. It is so much more comfortable to think that everything is relative. Claims to be *right* merely irritate.[1]

---

1 Curiously, the same standard is not required of some other religions, such as Islam. The iffy "facts" of Islam's early history are accepted without question or criticism, and little of its later history—so full of violent conquest and slaughter, mass slavery of the conquered, and radical discrimination against women and non-Muslims—is brought up to discredit it, as the defects of Catholics are repeatedly brought up against the Church.

Does this mean that the game is hopeless, and that we should not bother trying to put out one fire after another since there is always another pyromaniac just behind us? Because the opposition has a great archangel behind it, should we just acknowledge that combat is futile? Should we ignore the big and sticky historical issues? Certainly not. For one thing, if we straighten out even one person who has been duped by one lie, it is a victory for truth. If I convince two students out of fifty to revise their thinking on one of the issues covered in this book, it is a gain. We will never know, in fact, how many souls are actually touched by our defense of Catholic truth, because there is often a delayed reaction. (If the job were easy and everybody began to agree with us, what swelled heads we would get!)

If they have an archangel on their side (though most do not know it), we have a greater one on our side; and beyond St. Michael, we have the Woman Clothed with the Sun— and her very own Son, who is God. Seen this way, discouragement seems downright foolish. We have to inform ourselves about the true history of our Mother the Church, warts and all, and defend that truth with courtesy and competence whenever we are called to do so. For some this will mean public speaking and writing; for others, teaching religious education classes; for others, the teaching of children; for most, the occasional conversation with a friend who has it all wrong. We cannot go wrong, though, in learning and speaking the truth.

How are we to go about this? Read on for a few suggestions on confronting some of the lies discussed in this book.

APPENDIX 1

HOW TO ANSWER A LIE

I magine that someone says to you out of the blue, "You Catholics! You burned people for centuries just because they didn't agree with you." What do you say? If you're not well-informed, you might be tempted to agree sheepishly, since one hears such things so often. If you know your facts (as you must now, from reading this book), you might want to holler back with indignation, "We did *not!*"

But that will not get us very far. Knowledge is essential, but it must be properly presented. The only way to demonstrate that a lie *is* a lie is to have a reasoned discussion about it with your accuser. This is not as simple as it sounds, because relatively few people today seem willing (or able) either to reason or to follow an extended argument—particularly if it goes counter to the prejudices they have acquired. You can try saying something like, "You know, that's an interesting subject; I was reading something the other day about the burning of heretics. Let's have coffee tomorrow and talk about it."

This may have the result of opening a fruitful dialogue with a misinformed person, though sometimes it does not. So many times a student has asked a question in class about a lie or some other historical point, and because I want to be sure of my facts, I say I will do some research and answer the question in the next class. Often I spend a good deal of time researching the issue and planning my presentation, only to find at the next class that the student has lost interest or is not present to hear my answer.

Let us hope, however, that your interlocutor shows up at the coffee house. One of the best ways to proceed is to be Socrates: question the questioner and let him explain why he thinks Catholics were always burning people. What facts can he cite? (Often he has nothing concrete in mind; students and other young people will often refer quite seriously to movies as authorities, causing one to fear that they really cannot tell fact from fiction.) Explain why "tolerance," in the modern sense of "anything goes and it does not matter what one believes," did not exist in Christian times. On the contrary, people believed it was of the greatest importance that everyone believe what was true and what would bring him eternal life. Just as it was a crime to kill the body of a person, a crime for which death was often the penalty, so it was even more of a crime to kill the soul by destroying the virtues of faith, hope, and charity with false doctrine, because that destruction affected one's eternal destiny. It was thought that concern for the common good required that the heretic, teacher of false doctrine, should be prevented from corrupting souls. The best way to accomplish that was to show the heretic where he was wrong. If that did not work, he must at least be kept from spreading his spiritual poison; and in extreme cases, such as that of the suicide-promoting Cathars, he could be executed. Is this unreasonable? What do we do today with people who advocate committing crimes? The Catholic in this conversation is certainly not going to excuse those cases of injustice or actual cruelty that certainly existed; there were some harsh inquisitors and others in the past who richly deserved punishment. In all human affairs, no matter how good the cause, the fallible human beings involved are capable of both sin and error. Soldiers engaged in a perfectly just war, defending their country against unprovoked aggression, can be guilty of war crimes without discrediting the war.

So far you may get agreement on some of the points raised, but your questioner is more apt to bring up the issue of why you think the Catholic Church had the right to suppress heresy. He may object that that stance implies that the Catholic Church is the only true church of the thousands in existence, and nobody thinks that anymore; today everybody holds that everyone has the right to practice what he pleases. Now we are pretty far from merely discussing historical events; in fact, we are into apologetics.

But does the refutation of historical lies *always* have to lead back to the truth of the Church? Let us examine this question by looking at some of the other lies. The Crusades? They also raise the question of religious relativism: why should the Muslims not have had the Holy Land? After all, they venerate the sacred sites just as Christians do, and they have a right to have and to spread their own religion. The condemnation of Galileo? What authority did the Church have to decide that a scientist should be restricted in how he presented his findings? The supposed Catholic corruption of the pre-Reformation period? What difference does it make whether or not that existed, since the Protestants certainly had the right to set up their own religions, did they not, whether the Catholic Church was corrupt or not?

Fortunately or unfortunately, nearly all the lies discussed in this book, which are truly lies about *history*, lead back to basic questions about the *Catholic Faith*. This should give us an inkling that most of the lies were originally told by people who opposed *the Church herself*, not merely the interpretation of a historical happening. When we discuss historical lies, therefore, we must be prepared to go into the underlying presuppositions about God and faith. This is not so easy, but there is a wealth of apologetics resources available in print and online. (See Appendix 2 for some of these.)

In many cases, therefore, it does not seem possible to deal exclusively with *facts of history*—either because the lies about those facts are motivated by bias against the Church or because the lies ultimately raise the most basic questions about the Church. The Catholic historian (even the amateur historian) must therefore be prepared to be an apologist—a defender, not an apologizer. It is, of course, part of our Catholic vocation to be able to defend the Faith anyway, so this should come as no surprise. The classic rules of discussion pertain here, as they do in all conversations:

1. *Charity, first of all.* It must be out of concern for truth and the salvation of souls, not to score points by being

"right," that we get into controversy in the first place. Pray not just for the right words and arguments, but that the Holy Spirit will give you the grace of charity in everything you say.

2. *Define terms!* It is amazing—and discouraging—how often this ancient dictum is ignored (listen to any political debate) when it can all by itself provide the solution to an argument. Very often we find ourselves using words so loosely or inaccurately that only the vaguest concept can be drawn from them. Thus, one of the first things we will ask our discussion partner is what exactly he understands by the words he has used in condemning the Inquisition or the Crusades.

3. *Provide historical context for the issue under discussion.* It is important to realize how, though human nature remains the same, societal mentalities can change. The manner in which people of a given century see an issue will differ from that of people of a later or earlier time. This does not imply moral relativism, but simply an acknowledgment that historical circumstances affect perspective. A fifteenth-century Englishman and a modern historian might agree that the trial of Joan of Arc was a farce and her execution a crime—but the Englishman might also be glad that such a thorn in the side of the English army was out of the way, while the modern writer would see only the tragedy of the act. Understanding how people thought in the past makes their actions more comprehensible to later generations.

4. *See where you can both reach agreement.* "Do you agree with me that . . . ?" ought to lead to at least a few

non-controversial facts and help you to zero in on the one or two issues that are really sticking points.

5. *Be prepared to learn.* We can learn something in every discussion. It can often be quite illuminating to see how things we take for granted, whether in history or anything else, are seen quite differently by others. Sometimes that other perspective is an improvement on our own.

6. *Sum it all up.* "So I think we can both agree that . . ." is the best way to end a conversation on a disputed topic. Both of you should know where you stand, on what you agree, and what disagreements remain. Ideally, you will have corrected at least some of your acquaintance's misapprehensions about the Church; even one error corrected is a gain!

Blasphemy: The Most Evil Lie

In recent years, sinister historical lies that have nothing to do with fact have begun to surface and are now proliferating. They are turning up on television shows, in newspaper and magazine articles, in plays and films, and are characterized by unprecedented vulgarity and obscenity. I am referring to the barrage of lies about Our Lord, Our Lady, and the Apostles. Attacks on the Church have been common at all ages in her history, but obscene blasphemies against Jesus Christ Himself and His Mother have been, at the most, so rare in the mainstream media that most of us rarely or never heard of them. This is no longer so. Absurd accusations of immorality against Christ and Our Lady that, until very recently, would never have been tolerated in the media now assault Christian sensibilities from every direction—and there are no longer anti-blasphemy laws to check them because freedom of speech and freedom of the press are the reigning doctrines of democratic religion.

Should these lies be rationally examined and refuted by the ordinary Catholic?

The answer would seem to be no: first, because they are based on no evidence at all and therefore cannot be refuted by an appeal to the historical record; and secondly, because discussing them only gives them more publicity. The Father of Lies is the source of all lies, but usually indirectly; it is hard not to think that he is the *direct* source of this group of lies.

It is worth noticing that obscene blasphemies are rarely directed against the sacred figures of other religions. A cartoon lampooning Muhammad produces violent demonstrations and death threats against anyone who would dare mention the Prophet other than respectfully. This gives pause to the scurrilous journalist or screenwriter; he might really like to spew out vulgar fictions or lampoonings about Muhammad, but he is afraid of being assassinated. How about ridiculing a Jewish target—Moses, perhaps—or a Jewish hero of the Holocaust? No good. The screenwriter might end up in court, and he would at the very least be dogged by the damning accusation of anti-Semitism for the rest of his life. Eastern and neo-pagan religions he thinks too obscure, or too harmless (if not too virtuous), to mock. Very well. He will create the most obscene and disgusting falsehoods he can think of about Jesus Christ and His Mother. Certainly nothing bad will happen to him if he does so. In fact, he will profit.

How, then, should we react to this type of lie if we are

not to take it on directly? The last thing we want to do is to give it publicity, so we must be discreet. If we are on the firing line—as, for example, the curator of a museum who must decide whether an obscene and blasphemous painting should be exhibited; a publisher presented with the manuscript of a blasphemous novel (sure to be a bestseller!); the dean of a college where a blasphemous play is scheduled to open; or someone else in a position to fight the evil directly—we must of course do so. If we are members of an organization that combats defamation of Catholics (see Appendix 2), we will support efforts to fight blasphemy under its guidance. What we do not want to do is to raise the subject on our own, as we might often have occasion to do with the other lies. The nature of blasphemy is such that bringing it to the attention of someone who is unaware of it may have the effect of putting it into his imagination, where it does not belong. Dealing with blasphemy is thus somewhat like dealing with pornography; it is something to be resolutely shunned unless it is unavoidable. The best weapons here are fervent prayer and penance.

APPENDIX 2

Sources Used and Recommended

B elow I have listed mainly sources that were used but are not cited in the text. The sources for some quotations from primary texts have not been cited since they are taken from collections not widely accessible to the general reader. I have generally omitted sources of journal articles for the same reason, except when they are excerpted in works more widely available.

Preface

Keith Windschuttle, *The Killing of History: How Literary Critics and Social Theorists Are Murdering Our Past* (Encounter Books, 1996). This is referenced in Chapter Seven for its excellent extended discussion of the conquest of Mexico, but it is also a good introduction to modern theories that have been distorting the writing of history.

Chapter 1 – The Dark, Dark Ages

Douglas Bush, "The Renaissance and English Humanism: Modern Theories of the Renaissance," a 1939 lecture excerpted in Karl H. Dannenfeldt, ed., *The Renaissance— Medieval or Modern?* (D. C. Heath and Company, 1959).

The work in which Dr. Bush's lecture appears is one of a series called *Problems in European Civilization* published by D. C. Heath and Company. Each of these little books deals with a question much debated by historians and includes short essays by modern historians as well as relevant primary texts. Topics in the series range from the question of why the Roman Empire collapsed to the Cold War, with numerous volumes in between. As an introduction to a major historical topic they are extremely useful. Though the Heath Company no longer exists, the books are often available in used book stores or library book sales and are worth picking up if you like history.

Jules Michelet, "The Renaissance and the Discovery of the World and Man," from *Histoire de France,* excerpted in Denys Hay, ed., *The Renaissance Debate* (Holt, Rinehart and Winston, 1965). This is another collection of sources on the ongoing Renaissance controversy. The quotation from John Addington Symonds is also taken from this source.

Jacob Burckhardt, *The Civilization of the Renaissance in Italy* (The Modern Library, 1954). This book was originally written in 1860.

Norman F. Cantor, *Inventing the Middle Ages* (William Morrow and Company, 1991) .

John R. Hale *et al., Renaissance* (Time Incorporated, 1965).

Anne Freemantle, *The Age of Faith* (Time Incorporated, 1965).

Charles Homer Haskins, *The Renaissance of the Twelfth Century* (Harvard University Press, 1927). This is a very worthwhile work, engagingly written and full of detailed information about the undeniably progressive twelfth century. It is necessarily dated in spots but it is still an important text.

Christopher Dawson, *The Dividing of Christendom* (Sheed and Ward, 1965).

Lynn Thorndike's quip about Petrarch is from his article "Renaissance or Prerenaissance?" in the *Journal of the History of Ideas,* IV (1943), quoted in Dannerfeldt, *op. cit.*

Though I have not used it here, Régine Pernoud's *Those Terrible Middle Ages: Debunking the Myth* ought to be mentioned. Translated by Anne Englund Nash and published by Ignatius Press in 2000, it does a good job of confronting and demolishing a number of the lies about the period.

Chapter 2 – The Catholic Church, Enemy of Progress

For information about early Christian attitudes toward education, chapters IX and X of H. I. Marrou's classic *A History of Education in Antiquity* (Sheed and Ward, 1956) is invaluable. The detailed analyses of Greek and Roman schools and educational theories serve as excellent and useful background for the discussion of Christian education in its earliest forms.

For the revival of learning under Charlemagne there are many good histories; if you can only read one, Eleanor

Shipley Duckett's *Carolingian Portraits: A Study in the Ninth Century* (The University of Michigan Press, 1962) brings the period alive with great sympathy as well as learning and style.

Another popularly written older work, short but still very worth reading, is Charles Homer Haskins's *The Rise of Universities* (Cornell University Press, 1970). This was originally published in 1923 and has been reprinted many times since. Works used for Chapter One, such as Haskins's *The Renaissance of the Twelfth Century,* are also relevant here.

Chapter 3 – A Crusade Against the Truth

There are a number of excellent works on the Crusades. Apart from the general histories of Christendom by Henri Daniel-Rops and Warren Carroll, which include sections on the Crusades, Régine Pernoud's *The Crusaders* (Ignatius Press, 2003) is highly recommended. On the conditions of Christians in the areas conquered by the Arabs and Turks, see Bat Ye'or's *The Decline of Eastern Christianity under Islam: From Jihad to Dhimmitude* (Associated University Presses, 1996). A very recent work is *God's Battalions: The Case for the Crusades* by Professor Rodney Stark (Harper One, 2009.) This one is well worth reading, though the author cites secondary sources almost entirely; there are also some minor errors of fact, but one is willing to over-look them in a modern secular work that actually defends the Crusades. Good for Professor Stark! Lastly, my *Islam at the Gates* (Sophia Institute Press, 2008) deals with the struggles of Christendom against the Ottoman Turks.

For the section of this chapter in which various historians

are cited, the source is an article collection in the *Problems in European Civilization* series, referred to above under Chapter One. This one was published in 1964 and is entitled *The Crusades: Motives and Achievements.*

The Clinton speech can be found online at http://ecumene.org/clinton.htm.

Chapter 4 – The Sinister Inquisition

Arius is discussed in Henri Daniel-Rops's *The Church of the Apostles and Martyrs,* the first volume of his history of the Church in English translation (E. P. Dutton & Co., 1963).

On the Patarenes and Waldensians see Jeffrey B. Russell, editor, *Religious Dissent in the Middle Ages* (John Wiley & Sons, 1971). Chapters eight and nine on these heretics are translations from a German work by Herbert Grundmann and a French book by Raymonde Forville and Jean Rousset de Pina.

On the Albigensians, or Cathars, there are numerous sources, including a chapter in the book cited immediately above. An older but very readable work on the history of the Inquisition is E. Vacandard's *The Inquisition,* translated by Father Bertrand L. Conway (Longmans, Green, and Co., 1926). The reader should, however, keep in mind the age of the book when reading the chapter on the Spanish Inquisition, in view of the revisionist work now available on that subject. Another older but useful study is A. L. Maycock's *The Inquisition* (Harper & Brothers, 1927), which includes an introduction by Father Ronald Knox.

Hoffman Nickerson's *The Inquisition: A Political and Military Study of Its Establishment* (Kennikat Press, 1968) was first published in 1932. It is well-written and scholarly, though dated in spots, and it includes a preface by Hilaire Belloc that begins, "Nearly all the historical work worth doing at the present moment in the English language is the work of shoveling off heaps of rubbish inherited from the immediate past." That previous historical work, he states, suffered both from its anti-Catholicism and from not being thorough in its methods. Both the essay and Nickerson's work make for good reading, but again, be cautious about pre-1970s works on the Inquisition.

The Spanish Inquisition: A Historical Revision, by Henry Kamen, referred to in the text, was first published in 1965; a second edition came out in 1997, and that is probably the one to consult. I unwittingly acquired an abridged version of that second edition, which I cannot recommend. The related video is quite entertaining as well as informative.

Montaillou: The Promised Land of Error is the English title of a French work by LeRoy Ladurie (George Braziller, 1978). This is an exhaustively detailed investigation of a Cathar village, based on archaeology, biographies of the inhabitants of the village, and the testimony collected by the inquisitor Jacques Fournier.

On the military Albigensian Crusade, only touched on in the chapter, see the histories of the Church already mentioned. Joseph R. Strayer's *The Albigensian Crusades* is a classic account in English and it exists in several editions, as do more recent works on the topic.

Eugene D. Dukes, *Magic and Witchcraft in the Dark Ages* (University Press of America, 1996). This is an extraordinary book by a fine Catholic researcher, but unfortunately very hard to obtain; I got it on interlibrary loan. It details the reality of diabolical activity starting with the earliest Christian period, explores the forms it took in subsequent ages, and describes occult practices and their devotees. His somber conclusion, which addresses the situation in the United States today, is thought-provoking and unsettling, to say the least.

Chapter 5 – Science On Trial: The Catholic Church v. Galileo

Carl Becker's *The Heavenly City of the Eighteenth-Century Philosophers* (Yale University Press, 1963) is based on lectures given at Yale and first published in 1932. These gracefully written chapters give insight into the Enlightenment worship of nature and science and into the growth of the modern mentality. Worth reading.

Galileo's Daughter, by Dava Sobel (Penguin, 2000), is a fine account of the relationship between a difficult father and the daughter (a nun) on whom he so much depended, and a very interesting story.

Galileo, Science, and the Church, by Jerome J. Langford (University of Michigan Press, 1992) is a detailed analysis by a former Dominican, first published in 1966 and revised in 1971, of all facets of the Galileo case. The 1992 edition includes a postscript with additional information.

David Berlinski, *The Devil's Delusion: Atheism and its Scientific Pretensions* (Basic Books, 2009).

Chapter 6 – A Church Corrupted to the Core

Christopher Dawson's *The Dividing of Christendom* (Sheed and Ward, 1965) is an excellent summary of the many historical factors involved in the explosion that was the Reformation. Highly recommended, along with the relevant volumes in the history series by Carroll and Daniel-Rops.

A History of the Protestant Reformation in England and Ireland, by William Cobbett, revised by Francis Cardinal Gasquet (TAN Books, 1988). This is a photographic reproduction of an 1896 edition. Old and partisan as it is, this account gives valuable information about the effects of Protestant royal policies on individual localities studied by the author. Still very worthwhile reading.

Euan Cameron, *The European Reformation* (Clarendon Press, 1991). The quotations from this excellent study that are included in the chapter give an idea of the work. A really good source for details about the Reformation in Europe.

Eamon Duffy, *The Stripping of the Altars: Traditional Religion in England 1400-1580* (Yale University Press, 1992). It is hard to praise this work too much for its scholarship and for the comprehensive picture it gives of the Catholic Faith in pre-Reformation England and its impact on the lives and customs of ordinary people. Excellent in every way.

The quotation from Pierre Janelle is from another one of those useful little collections of historians' writings on a given historical topic from various perspectives. This one, edited by W. Stanford Reid and published in 1968 by Holt, Rinehart, and Winston in their *European Problem Studies* series, is *The Reformation: Revival or Revolution?* It includes articles by Catholic historians such as Father P. H. Grisar, S.J. and Hugh Ross Williamson, among others.

I have cited James J. Walsh's *The Century of Columbus* (Catholic Summer School Press, 1914) even though there is much in it that needs updating, because in some areas it is the most accessible source of information. With his medical background, Walsh was able to go into topics, such as the use of anesthesia and the details of hospital care, that are hard to find information about elsewhere. Moreover, both this work and *The Thirteenth, Greatest of Centuries* by the same author are well written and full of fascinating material.

Sometimes a good historical novel can give a better "feel" for a time period and its main developments than scholarly works. Readers interested in the dramatic playing-out of various stages of the Reformation in England and in the characters involved cannot do better than to read the historical novels of Hugh Benson. Monsignor Benson was the son of an Archbishop of Canterbury and was highly educated in English history. Combined with his later conversion to Catholicism and his literary gifts, this background gave him a unique perspective on the Reformation. His novels depict historical figures and events vividly and accurately, and above all with sympathy. He could "get inside" his characters, no matter what side of the issues they were on, and show them to us in all their complexity, as religious and political revolt swirled around them. Above all, he knew the historical setting thoroughly, beginning with pre-Reformation England. The books should be read in chronological order if possible, though unfortunately several titles are out of print and difficult to find. The novel that deals with the religious situation under Henry VIII is *The King's Achievement,* in which the characters of King Henry VIII, St. Thomas More, Thomas Cromwell, and other historical figures are well presented in the context of a gripping story. *The Queen's Tragedy* is a fictionalized biography of Queen Mary Tudor with an interesting perspective on Mary, Philip II, the young Elizabeth, and others of the period. *Come Rack! Come Rope!* is perhaps the best-known of Benson's novels in this country because of its printing as a mass market paperback. Unfortunately, that edition is considerably condensed from the original work, though it is still well worth reading. It is one of two works set in the reign of Elizabeth, the second being the fine *By What Authority.* Finally, the reign of Charles II, who restored the Stuart monarchy following the death of the Puritan dictator Oliver Cromwell and his son, is the subject of *Oddsfish!*, a favorite expression of Charles. The scene of the King's deathbed conversion has often been reproduced in other works. All these books are the fruit of meticulous research by the author, who frequently had them checked for historical accuracy before publication. The early ones in particular give a vivid picture of religious conditions in England on the eve of the English Reformation.

Chapter 7 – A Black and Expedient Legend

Tree of Hate is cited in the chapter. Keith Windschuttle's *The Killing of History* (Encounter Books, 1996) discusses a number of controversial historical topics in several chapters, of which only one deals with the Spanish-Aztec confrontation. It is worth consulting for the details provided about the appalling religious practices of the Aztecs—and about the modern theories that allow historians to whitewash them.

Warren H. Carroll's *Our Lady of Guadalupe and the*

Conquest of Darkness (Christendom Press, 1993) is a short but detailed treatment of the Conquest. Highly recommended.

The Spanish Struggle for Justice in the Conquest of America (Little, Brown, and Company, 1965) by Columbia University professor Lewis Hanke is an excellent short treatment of an important topic. It was originally published in 1946 and may be dated in places but is still worth reading.

A classic film, *The Mission,* is a drama based on the actual history of Spanish missionary work with the Stone-Age Guarani Indians on the border between Uruguay and Paraguay, highlighting the great musical talent those Indians possessed. It is recommended, with some reservations, as a good introduction to the Jesuit invention of the *reductions* (native mission-plantations), which were used to protect such Indians from exploitation. The only really jarring note is the scene near the end of the film that has Jesuit priests fighting their expulsion with guns; it didn't happen.

The Lost Paradise: The Jesuit Republic in South America, by Philip Caraman, S.J. (Dorset Press, 1975) is an account of the *reductions* and what happened to them.

Chapter 8 – And There Are More . . .

On Pope Pius XII and the Jews, a number of books have recently appeared, among them Rabbi David G. Dalin, *The Myth of Hitler's Pope: Pope Pius XII and His Secret War against Nazi Germany* (Regnery Publishing, 2005); Margherita Marcione's *Did Pope Pius XII Help the Jews?* (Paulist Press, 2007), one of several books by this author devoted to defending Pope Pius; and Robert J. Rychlak's *Hitler, the War, and the Pope* (Our Sunday Visitor, 2000).

A fascinating history of the role of secret intelligence during World War II, particularly with reference to the German resistance that aimed at the overthrow of the Hitler regime, is *The Unseen War in Europe*, by John H. Waller (Random House, 1996). There is a chapter entitled "Operation X: The Vatican Connection" that details the role of the Church and of the Pope personally in promoting resistance to the Nazis.

One of the best sources for ongoing work on Pius XII, as well as for the lies discussed at the end of Appendix 1 and many other issues, is the Catholic League for Religious and Civil Rights. In addition to its print newsletter, the League's website, http://www.catholicleague.org/, provides frequently updated information on many questions of concern to Catholics. Highly recommended.

On women being historically oppressed—indeed absent from history, especially in the Middle Ages—Régine Pernoud's *Women in the Days of the Cathedrals* is a fine antidote. The book explores the various roles taken by women and gives details on the lives of some of the most interesting ones.

On the very large question of the Church and slavery there are many sources. A fairly recent and accessible one is Joel S. Panzer's *The Popes and Slavery* (Alba House, 1996.)

Appendix 1 – How to Answer a Lie

Anyone likely to engage in apologetics should assemble a small library of works on topics likely to come up in discussions. (A book on logical argument would be useful too.) The magazine *This Rock,* published by Catholic Answers, is very useful for ideas on apologetics. Information is available from www.catholic.com.

ABOUT THE AUTHOR

Diane Moczar, Ph.D., teaches history at Northern Virginia Community College. She is the author of several books, including *Islam at the Gates*, about Europe's wars with Ottoman Turks, and *Ten Dates Every Catholic Should Know*.

Saint Benedict Press, founded in 2006, is the parent company for a variety of imprints including TAN Books, Catholic Courses, Benedict Bibles, Benedict Books, and Labora Books. The company's name pays homage to the guiding influence of the Rule of Saint Benedict and the Benedictine monks of Belmont Abbey, North Carolina, just a short distance from the company's headquarters in Charlotte, NC.

Saint Benedict Press is now a multi-media company. Its mission is to publish and distribute products reflective of the Catholic intellectual tradition and to present these products in an attractive and accessible manner.

TAN Books was founded in 1967, in response to the rapid decline of faith and morals in society and the Church. Since its founding, TAN Books has been committed to the preservation and promotion of the spiritual, theological and liturgical traditions of the Catholic Church. In 2008, TAN Books was acquired by Saint Benedict Press. Since then, TAN has experienced positive growth and diversification while fulfilling its mission to a new generation of readers.

TAN Books publishes over 500 titles on Thomistic theology, traditional devotions, Church doctrine, history, lives of the saints, educational resources, and booklets.

For a free catalog from Saint Benedict Press
or TAN Books, visit us online at
saintbenedictpress.com • tanbooks.com
or call us toll-free at
(800) 437-5876